Further Praise for *Your Retirement Smile*

Tim and Mart opened my eyes to how the financial industry really works. As a practicing orthodontist, I was extremely proficient in my field but woefully ignorant when it came to my finances. The team at Macro Wealth Management has leveled the playing field, giving doctors the tools they need to build wealth.

—Dr. Tom Shannon, Grandville, MI

A number of years ago, I was invited to attend a "retirement planning lecture." I only attended to not offend my friend. When I returned home that night, I told my wife, "I'm not sure, but I think I just listened to something that will completely change our life in retirement. I was blown away." Since that time, I have worked with Macro Wealth Management and I no longer worry about what my income level will be once I retire. With their strategies—that are not your cookie-cutter, in-the-box, standard ways—I know I will be able to count on my guaranteed income level in retirement.

—Dr. Bill Dischinger, Lake Oswego, OR
key opinion leader, Ormco Corporation

Mart and Tim's data-driven approach to financial "treatment" planning is as intelligent as it is important for us all to hear. I wish I would have heard this information a long time ago!

—Dr. Jamie Reynolds, Novi, MI
founder of OrthoFi

Mart and Tim have been instrumental in helping my family to be on the road to achieving our financial goals. From the very beginning, they have taken a "macro" approach to ensure that not only are we investing our money wisely but that we have systems in place to ensure that our family will have financial stability in the event of any unforeseen circumstances. This is not the sale of a "get rich quick" system or a magical "product," instead, this is a careful approach that truly is tailored to help you achieve and maintain financial success!

—Todd Erdman, Wheeling, IL
dental attorney

Mart and Tim are helping investors in general and dentists in particular live the life of their dreams in retirement. They debunk much of the conventional "wisdom" of high-cost, transaction-hungry Wall Street firms and focus on the benefits of planning and discipline. They are consummate professionals in a world often dominated by salespeople.

—Patrick Sweeny, Glastonbury, CT
principal and cofounder, Symmetry Partners, LLC

After powering through the Tony Robbins book, I think Your Retirement Smile *is a much more understandable read!*

—Dr. John Foley, NC

Mart and Tim have sculpted a tremendous pathway to understanding your retirement and a direct line to confidence about your future.

—John Pobanz, South Ogden, UT
clinical professor at the University of Nevada Dental School

Nothing short of masterfully awesome!

—Dr. David Allen, Wheaton, IL

I was a marketing and sales professional in the insurance industry for forty-five years, but even that did not prevent me from making some very poor financial decisions.

While serving as the regional VP for a Midwest-based life insurance company, I met Tim and Mart. Over the course of a few years, Tim and I formed a personal friendship in addition to a very strong business relationship. I finally asked Tim to show me his "process" and, from that encounter, my wife and I became his clients and are we ever glad we did ... our only regret is that we didn't meet Tim earlier! Working with Tim, we are VERY well-positioned in our retirement. I have encouraged both of my sons to seek out Tim and pay heed to his extremely valuable advice.

—Robert Ley, IL

From the very start of my career, I knew regardless of what anyone told me, I wanted to live at the same financial level through my retirement years as I would through my work years. I didn't know how I was going to achieve this goal until I sat down for a meeting with Mart and Tim, friends I've known for years. Macro Wealth Management has enabled me to achieve this goal. This company practices what they preach, and they truly care for their clients. As I sat with Mart and Tim, I did not see salesmen, I saw genuine men who wanted to help me. It has been a pleasure working with them through the years, and I know I can always count on them.

—Dr. Rob Girgis, Woodridge, IL
former president of the Illinois Society of Orthodontists

I have worked with Tim for over fifteen years. In the process of those fifteen years, I have leaned on Tim to assist in every financial decision I have made. From buying vacation property in Park City, Utah, to buying my family business, to making additions to our home and, for sure, building my own strip center for my business twelve years ago, Tim has been there every step of the way. What makes his Treatment Plan different from every other advisor I have worked with in my twenty-plus years of working is the fact that it challenges you to enjoy your life and your earnings now while you are young all the while creating the possibility of living a full-bodied life once you retire. Tim and his Treatment Plan have allowed me to sleep soundly knowing that my family will truly enjoy our best years now, all the while celebrating our golden years with more protection and security than we ever dreamed of. Tim has made my life and my family's life better because of our financial security, and it all goes back to that model that is proven, tested, and solid. Every family should be built on a strong foundation ... our financial future is for sure sound. Thanks, Tim!

—Robert Woolsey, Peoria, IL
president of Jones Bros. Jewelers

Your Retirement Smile *is a refreshing new look on what truly matters regarding retirement planning. It is uniquely and creatively written with new financial ideas and substance. It is not laden with lots of investment or product hype. It zeros in on many facets of financial life, which many financial planners and financial institutions do not consider or disregard. If your current planning makes you feel like you are doing all the right things, but you don't seem to be getting ahead, this book is a must-read. Once you start reading this book, you will not want to put it down. Each page is filled with life-changing ideas for a better and more reassuring financial life. Enjoy!*

—Lenny Martin, CLU, ChFC, RHU

Mart McClellan, DDS, MS, is an expert at creating beautiful and lasting smiles! Now, he has teamed up with Mr. Tim Streid, CLU, to help create lasting smiles for dental professionals into their retirement years. Their combined financial expertise and knowledge of the unique financial position of dental professionals has led to the creation of an invaluable Financial Treatment Plan for retirement. As consultants in the dental field, we know that dental school rarely sets new doctors up for financial and business success. It is a missing part of the curriculum that most doctors desperately need. Through the implementation of evidence-based processes, a macro-economic foundation, and sound financial coaching, doctors following their Financial Treatment Plan can set themselves up for ultimate financial stability in retirement. This information is not only invaluable for dental professionals but for anyone seeking to maximize their financial security in retirement. This is a resource that we will undoubtedly share with every client that we work with!

—Manon Newell, MD
COO Systemized Orthodontics Consulting Group

YOUR
retirement
SMILE

DR. MART McCLELLAN   TIM STREID

YOUR

retirement

SMILE

THE TREATMENT PLAN FOR

PAY-CUT PREVENTION

IN YOUR GOLDEN YEARS

Advantage®

Published by Advantage, Charleston, South Carolina.
Member of Advantage Media Group.

ADVANTAGE is a registered trademark, and the Advantage colophon is a trademark of Advantage Media Group, Inc.

Printed in the United States of America.

10 9 8 7 6 5 4 3 2 1

ISBN: 978-1-59932-956-7
LCCN: 2019911008

Book design by Jamie Wise.

Advantage Media Group is proud to be a part of the Tree Neutral® program. Tree Neutral offsets the number of trees consumed in the production and printing of this book by taking proactive steps such as planting trees in direct proportion to the number of trees used to print books. To learn more about Tree Neutral, please visit www.treeneutral.com.

Advantage Media Group is a publisher of business, self-improvement, and professional development books and online learning. We help entrepreneurs, business leaders, and professionals share their Stories, Passion, and Knowledge to help others Learn & Grow. Do you have a manuscript or book idea that you would like us to consider for publishing? Please visit advantagefamily.com or call 1.866.775.1696.

We would like to dedicate this book to our wives, Lindsey and Julie, who have been there every step of the way. They held down the fort and cared for our children while we were away, lecturing across the country, attending meetings, or meeting with clients—assistance that was invaluable to our success. We could not have done it without you! Although our children weren't always aware of the help we were providing to our clients, we thank them for their hugs, kisses, and smiles when we returned home from our trips and their support through the years. We would also like to acknowledge all of our clients who have embraced our information. They have seen firsthand that there is a much better way to create incredible life enjoyment for themselves and their families. It is a magical moment when our clients first realize they can retire on their terms with much more income, more guarantees, less risk, and no additional out-of-pocket outlay. This cannot be done in the traditional world of personal finance, which is why we have written this book.

CONTENTS

• • •

NOBODY LIKES A PAY CUT

• • •

As you walk down the fairway of life, you must smell the roses, for you only get to play one round.

—BEN HOGAN

It is safe to say that no one likes to take a pay cut—*ever*. Yet, almost every American and dentist will take one in retirement! For many, it will be a big pay cut. This is why the information in this book is so important for you, your family, and the charities to which you want to contribute. You are about to embark on a financial journey that will change how you approach your financial decision making. If you can remain open minded, your financial life will forever be transformed.

Our objective is to put a smile on your face when it comes to retirement and remove the trepidations (or frowns) that so many have when they enter their golden years. It will likely make you feel a bit uncomfortable at times. Why? Because almost everything you have been told about being financially successful is a half truth or misinformation. It will be frustrating because you will ask yourself many times, *Why haven't I been told this in the past?* or think to yourself, *I thought there might be a better way.* The good news is that it is not too late to implement these strategies and become significantly wealthier, have more free time to spend with your family and friends, and have the ability to make a great contribution to society through charitable giving!

Since time is a limited resource, it is an extremely valuable asset. Hence, having more free time is what everyone wants. In her book, *The Top Five Regrets of the Dying,* Australian nurse Bronnie Ward writes that one of the regrets shared among those who are dying is that they wish they hadn't worked so hard. In her research, family and relationship expert Hellen Chen found that "the deepest regret that I have heard has been men and women missing out on the most important part of life: the quality of their relationship in a marriage and/or with their children." The beauty of the information within this book is that it creates so much security now and retirement income for the future that it expands time, giving people more time for the important things in their lives.

Pick up any magazine article on money, listen to the financial gurus or entertainers on the radio or television, or read financial advice online and you will believe that people fall into two groups when it comes to money: savers and spenders, with spenders having a more negative connotation.

The truth is money is not an either/or thing. It is not now *or* later. It is not all *or* nothing. When it comes to your money, you *can* have your cake and eat it too. You can save *and* spend. You can invest for the future *and* enjoy your life in the present. You can enjoy life to its fullest during your working years and have 100 percent income replacement when you retire. How? By following a macroeconomic financial process that allows you to enjoy your life now *and* retire without taking a pay cut or having the fear of running out of money. This is how we create your retirement smile!

In the dental world, the 2010 report on retirement, published by the American Dental Association (ADA), shows that dentists take, on average, a 50 percent pay cut the moment they retire. When we meet dentists across the country, we find this number to be about right. Think of this in terms dentists know well: taking a test. If you are studying to become a dentist and you get a 50 percent grade, you are failing. It is unacceptable. So, if you retire with a 50 percent drop in income, didn't your financial plan just fail? The answer is a resounding yes, yet that is the path most dentists and Americans will be on until they read this book.

No dentist wants to fail or struggle when it comes to their personal finances. The acceptance of anything less than full income replacement in retirement is less than successful. Oftentimes, traditional financial advisors[1] will justify the reduced income, such as 70 percent of your preretirement income, by saying that is all you need, but is that what you want? If you could position yourself to retire with full income replacement, at no additional out-of-pocket cost to you, wouldn't you want that? Instead of receiving a failing grade in personal finance you would receive an A+. Who would you rather be: the stellar financial student with minimal worries in retirement or the one who does what everyone else is doing and in retirement has less income, more risk, and increased stress?

Individuals make financial decisions every day, whether it is buying a car or house, paying off student loans or consumer debt, paying for a child's college expenses, purchasing an insurance product,

---

1   We will reference traditional advisors many times in this book. These advisors include certified financial planners, nationwide dental advisory firms, online forums and blogs, radio personalities, financial magazines, stockbrokers, accountants, lawyers, and life insurance agents.

saving for retirement, or making various investment decisions, just to name a few. Each of these decisions is made at specific points in our lifetime with different advisors, who usually have differing opinions. We call these decisions *microeconomic* decisions. The truth is, however, a benign decision, such as how you pay your mortgage, not only affects the mortgage on your house (micro), but it also affects many other aspects of your financial life from a *macroeconomic* perspective. It is essential to understand this interaction, something that will be explained later in the book.

The big question is, How do you know what is right? If you are making every financial decision from a microeconomic viewpoint only, then by default, you lose the added benefits and value that a macroeconomic approach to your financial decision making brings to the table. Ignoring the macroeconomic impact of a financial decision causes individuals to unknowingly lose hundreds of thousands of dollars, if not millions, over their lifetime. This is why most dentists are only retiring on half of their preretirement income.

Purchasing financial products in the wrong way will not only cost you a ton of money, but the misunderstood strategies that are sold with these products will prove to be even more costly today and in retirement. Touted traditional financial strategies, such as the compounding of interest in a taxable environment, excessive tax deferrals for retirement plan contributions, or the acceleration of debt repayment, are just a few of the many weak recommendations made by advisors across the country. Each of them will contribute to a disappointing retirement from an income standpoint. Wrong products with the wrong strategies create a significant pay cut in retirement.

Reading this book for the first time may make you feel uncomfortable. Your unease will be due to the fact that you will recognize many of these traditional strategies as ones that you are presently employing in your current financial plan. One of the many purposes of this book is to help you discover, through an evidence-based process, why these strategies are weak. At the same time, you will be introduced to a comprehensive process and framework for evaluating financial decisions from an economic basis that will allow a paradigm shift and make your financial life significantly better.

Most dentists we work with enjoy their profession, but as much as they do, it is safe to say they will retire at some point. It is not a matter of *if* you will retire as much as it is *what kind* of retirement you will have: a very fruitful retirement, or one that only has some fruit on the retirement tree. An abundant, fruitful tree enables you to continue working because you want to and not because you have to.

The hard facts are that only 5 percent of dentists can retire comfortably.[2] This is a shocking number. The vast majority of dentists have no idea that their present situations can be so much better. One question you should ask yourself is, If all the financial information promoted by traditional advisors, the media, online forums and blogs, financial institutions, corporations, and our parents/friends/colleagues is so good, why aren't more dentists able to retire successfully? Also, why are seniors running out of money in retirement? The answer is that they don't have a strategic, macro-Financial Treatment Plan. This book is the Financial Treatment Plan for pay-cut prevention in your golden years!

---

2   "2010 Survey on Retirement and Investment," American Dental Association, https://ebusiness.ada.org/productcatalog/452/Dentistry/2010-Survey-on-Retirement-and-Investment-Downloadable-SC/SRI-2010D#.

• • • • • • • • • • • • • • • • • • •

Mart

I'm from a middle-class family that has their roots in the Midwest. My father was the first to graduate from college. As a young child, I was raised in West Virginia and then, as a teenager, I moved to Connecticut. I was recruited to play golf and basketball at DePauw University, where I went on two mission trips to Kenya and Guatemala and discovered dentistry. My interest in dentistry led me to Northwestern University Dental School and, finally, to the University of Michigan orthodontic residency program.

Like most Americans, financial planning was never a significant topic of conversation for the first thirty years of my life, other than my grandparents talking about saving money because they only had pea soup to eat during the Depression years! After graduating from my orthodontic residency with a ton of student loan debt, my wife and I engaged some financial advisors, who gave traditional advice. I thought they were doing the right things with our money until one day, after an annual review, our advisor recommended that we switch from one product we bought from him years before to another product. We thought that what we had purchased years before was appropriate, but now it was not? It did not seem or smell right, but how were we to know?

Maybe it was divine intervention, but just as I was about to finalize that decision with my traditional advisor, I met Tim. I didn't know Tim from Adam. He was advising one of my dental school classmates who said Tim had helped him out a lot. When we first met, Tim said he could actually measure financial decisions with a macro-economic system he used and verify what option would give me greater output from a rate of return and benefits standpoint. I asked him if he could take the product my wife and I had bought three years earlier and compare it to the change our advisor was now recommending. At that point Tim had no skin in the game other than showing me his powerful system.

Tim showed me clearly, with a side-by-side comparison, that what we had purchased years before was the more appropriate path for us. The new recommendation was nothing more than a way for our old advisor to churn the account for a commission. That single decision to keep in place what my wife and I had originally purchased changed our financial life forever. It also allowed us to do things we would not have been able to do if we had made that switch. From that point, we were Tim's clients for the next seven years.

• • • • • • • • • • • • • • • • • • •

• • • • • • • • • • • • • • • • • • •

Tim

During the time I advised Mart and Lindsey, the stock market crashed after the dot-com era and the September 11 terror attack on the twin towers. Despite this, Mart's financial life was thriving. On the other hand, many of

Mart's friends' and colleagues' financial situations were not as good, due to the volatile stock market. It was at that time that Mart and I made the decision to share our information with the dental community. We started doing some speaking engagements together and writing joint articles in national publications. Our message started gaining some traction, and we had the opportunity to lecture both nationally and internationally.

That's when we decided to take things to the next level and start our advisory firm, Macro Wealth Management, in 2004. It's hard to believe it's been fifteen years now.

• • • • • • • • • • • • • • • • • • • •

Our Financial Treatment Plan is based on the theories of economist Robert Castiglione, who developed his model in 1980. The most powerful part of his system is that it has stood the test of time through good and bad markets and ever-changing tax laws and interest rate environments. Successful planning comes from plans that work under even the worst-case scenario, and this is what Bob Castiglione created. It would be safe to say that anything better than a worst-case scenario is fantastic!

With backgrounds in financial planning and dentistry, which is our unique value proposition, we established Macro Wealth Management, using a comprehensive financial model as the foundation for our advisory practice. Because of our unique backgrounds, the lion's share of our work is done in the dental profession, but the concepts work for everyone.

Dental school offers very little, if any, training in personal finance or practice management. When you graduate from dental school, you are Little Red Riding Hood, and the financial advisor is the wolf dressed as Grandma. The wolf thinks you have or will have a lot of money due to the word *doctor* being part of your title. The truth is you may have as much as half a million dollars in student loan debt and no money to buy a home or a practice.

This is the typical plight of a new dental graduate. As a new dentist, you have no idea how to start a practice or run a business, let alone how to deal with your personal finances. Your focus becomes being a good dentist, which is fantastic, but this comes at the expense of personal wealth building.

Because you are so focused on building your business, you begin to lose sight of the personal financial management side of the equation. Instead, you hire a financial advisor or certified financial planner, whose primary focus is selling products or developing plans that are linear in fashion. You buy in, pay the significant fees, and get a financial plan in a three-ring binder that is mostly boilerplate.

That three-ring binder pretty much just sits on your shelf and collects dust. Implementation of the plan, which is essential for success, may not even occur, as the planning fee has already been paid. If a product is purchased, it is often done in a very ineffective manner with no coordination or integration of the product in the overall Financial Treatment Plan. Time goes by and you meet with your advisor here and there. Then, three years later the stock market is going crazy and your advisor wants to get together. Your advisor says you need to replace what you bought three years earlier because the stock market is now booming and you don't want to miss out. This tactic is known as the weak FOMO (fear of missing out) strategy. If you move to the new investment at this time, however, you will buy into a rising market, which is the opposite of what you should be doing. Confronted with this situation, you don't know what is right, nor do you have the time to research it, so you buy again. This is the normal cycle of financial distress in which most dentists find themselves.

Many dentists who are approaching retirement today, or are actually retired, are leading what we refer to as quiet lives of economic desperation. They may look good on the outside, but when you look at their personal finances, it is obvious that they are struggling or distressed due to the enormous uncertainty of the future.

The struggle or stress that the vast majority of dentists experience is resolved when a holistic Financial Treatment Plan is introduced into their lives. It is not just about looking at a retirement plan or investments. It is also about analyzing hard assets, such as real estate, your dental practice, gold, silver, cryptocurrencies such as Bitcoin, artwork, and so on. Your liquidity also plays a significant role in the equation, as does how you are protected with your auto, homeowners, and liability insurance coverage. It also takes into consideration your disability and life insurance, your wills and trust, and your debt situation. *Every* decision you make within that Financial Treatment Plan will always impact something else within the plan. If you don't have a framework from which to measure financial decisions, then you won't know where the problems or inefficiencies exist. They will go unseen. A Financial Treatment Plan provides a macroeconomic picture of your financial life. Its presence is the underlying factor that allows you to achieve a successful retirement versus one that is mediocre at best.

Many dentists head into retirement knowing they are in trouble, but not wanting to admit it. Other dentists think they are totally fine because they have accumulated a lot of money. However, many of these dentists are also in trouble if they don't have a distribution plan in place for their income. No matter how much money you have, without an efficient distribution plan in place, you are still going to take a pay cut in retirement or not live life to its fullest. Even if you have been extremely successful and have done all the right things from a traditional financial standpoint, you will still not be doing as well as you could be doing because the track you are on is not efficient.

It does not have to be that way.

Dentists make a great income, which is certainly above the income of the average American household. The problem for dentists is not that they don't make enough money. They make plenty of money. The problem is that their money is not positioned appropriately.

Whether we make $50,000 a year or $500,000 a year, we all have a finite amount of money that will enter our lives during our lifetime. Every dollar that comes in is precious. We have to understand how money works and how to best make money work for us. With that being said, each dollar has a specific position at a particular time for ultimate efficiency. The question you should ask yourself is, Am I confident that my money is positioned perfectly for maximum output to ensure more benefits and multiple income streams in retirement?

Most dentists believe that a successful retirement is based solely on how big their pile of assets is at retirement. There is actually a book published in the world of personal finance that asks, "What's your number?" for retirement, as if that has anything to do with a successful retirement.[3] According to a *Journal of Clinical Orthodontics* survey, respondents felt that $2,000,000 was the threshold for being ready for retirement.[4] What is your number or how big does your

---

3   Lee Eisenberg, *The Number: A Completely Different Way to Think About the Rest of Your Life (New York: Free Press, 2006).*

4   Jeremiah Sturgill and Jae Park, "Changes in Orthodontists' Retirement Planning and Practice Operations Due to the Recent Recession," *Journal of Clinical Orthodontics* 49, no. 4 (April 2015): 240–8.

pile of assets have to be for you to achieve the retirement of your dreams? Would $10,000,000 be enough? Would you be content with that number?

Most dentists would be extremely happy to be in that position, but let's not forget that life is relative. It is safe to say that if you are a dentist with that much money saved for retirement, your income was probably upward of $500,000 a year for the better part of your career, maybe closer to over $1 million a year.

Let's assume you were earning $500,000 a year in your practice, before retirement. In the traditional world of financial planning, the $10,000,000 of retirement assets will deliver $300,000 of retirement income using a 3 percent safe withdrawal strategy (explained later). Now, $300,000 is a lot of money, but you were making a half million dollars before you retired. That means you will have a huge 40 percent pay cut in retirement! Some may think that $300,000 in retirement is more than enough income, but if you could have more, would that be a better result?

Our view is that if you were to position your money correctly and use the *same* dollars (we're not saying put more money in; we're saying use the same dollars to do more), your retirement income could be $500,000 or more, as opposed to $300,000. That's right. Simply by reworking the money in your Financial Treatment Plan, substantially more retirement income is possible. Why wouldn't you want that?

If you were to take a 50 percent pay cut in retirement, regardless of your previous income, the lifestyle you were accustomed to while engaged in your career would be reduced significantly in your golden years. Therein lies the problem, because no matter what income level you achieve, it is impossible to live the same lifestyle on half of the money. This problem would be further compounded if no guarantees were built in to your plan. Hence, having more retirement income resolves this problem whether you are a spender or a saver!

Think about the opportunities you would have if you had full income replacement in retirement that was inflation protected. One, your lifestyle would not change. Two, if you didn't feel you needed or wanted the additional dollars, you could invest them back into your Financial Treatment Plan and leave a larger legacy for loved ones and charities. These dollars could be used to spoil grandkids or pay for their college educations. You could take your family on vacations beyond their wildest dreams. If you were to have $200,000 in annual income that you don't need, you could donate it to a charity or to a cause you are passionate about. With full income replacement in retirement, you have the opportunity to do all of these things because you *want* to do them. That extra income would give you security, options, and flexibility that would not be possible with less income. Most importantly, you would have the greatest gift of all: financial peace of mind.

Almost all the financial information that we are exposed to from the many different outlets soliciting us is misinformation. It is voluminous. This doesn't mean it is *totally* wrong. It may be right from a *micro* standpoint, but it is wrong from a *macro* standpoint. When it is wrong from a macroeconomic standpoint, your resulting income and enjoyment will be less. This is the suboptimal nature of conventional wisdom!

This concept of micro versus macro is also true for those dentists who decide to manage their own finances or follow the path of their successful parents. Managing your financial future in this way is a guarantee of less income, something that most people do not want. As successful as some of our parents are, the concept of income replacement in retirement is something most have never discussed and they, too, may be taking a pay cut in their golden years! This will be discussed in more detail in chapter 3.

We have yet to come across a single instance where our Financial Treatment Plan did not provide more retirement income and benefits. When a dentist uses a macroeconomic system to analyze and verify each financial decision, a financially successful retirement can be accomplished. This is evidence-based planning at its best.

Our hope is that everyone who reads this book discovers a new mind-set when it comes to making financial decisions. We want you to recognize that the same-old-same-old or cookie-cutter approach to finances does not have to be accepted, nor should it be. Also, we want you to have the curiosity and the desire to seek out a different life when it comes to retirement. But we don't want you to just read this book. Instead, we want you to take action and find a better way to make your money work for you and your family as you go forward.

Your mind-set will certainly have to change because as you read the following pages, you will realize that what you are presently doing will not get you to full income replacement in retirement. The following material has stood the test of time in different economic environments and will encourage a paradigm shift. This information will not only have a significant impact on you and your family but also on society if you have a charitable intent.

Chapter 1

THE FIGHT FOR YOUR MONEY

• • •

All wealth is a product of knowledge.

—GEORGE GILDER

When building or creating wealth, there are two prevailing economic principles of money that can be followed: accumulation and acceleration. The accumulation principle focuses on simple math and ways to accumulate and compound your wealth over time. The acceleration principle emphasizes achieving exponential growth through strategies that allow more than one use for every dollar and each use of your dollar creates a new rate of return with additional benefits. In essence, the acceleration principle keeps your money in motion and accelerates your wealth over time. Which principle do you follow: accumulation or acceleration?

Where do these principles originate and which are the entities that decide the rules in the world of finance? There are actually three: the government, financial institutions, and corporations. We refer to these three entities as the rainmakers. A viable, capitalistic society requires the presence of all three entities. We would not want to live in a society where any one of these entities did not exist.

Let's look at a situation in which all three of these entities are intertwined within our economy. The government exists and thrives on a large and continuing tax revenue base. In an effort to spur the economy, the government may create tax breaks or credits for real estate developers and investors to build low-income housing for the poor. This, in turn, puts people to work and creates revenue and profits for the developer and all the subcontractors and suppliers employed in the real estate project. Corporations and businesses further benefit from the new construction as individual homeowners seek to buy furnishings and appliances for their new home. Financial institutions also benefit from the new mortgages and various insurance coverage acquired and purchased by the new homeowners.

The scenario just described creates a win-win-win situation for all three of the rainmakers. The initial tax benefit offered by the government should increase profits generated by corporations and financial institutions and drive tax revenues. Also, when people are employed, the income and payroll tax base is maintained or increases with a growing and productive economy. Corporations and businesses, including their individual shareholders and owners, are happy with the increased sales revenues and business profits. Finally, financial institutions continue to count their money due to the interest and fees generated from the new loans and insurance premiums they collect. As shown, all three of the rainmakers can work together to create and support a vibrant economy.

With this in mind, however, let's not lose sight of the rainmakers' ultimate objective, which is to take and control of as much of our money as possible. Although we are in a fight with the rainmakers for our money, we don't have to live by the rules they create for consumers. Their rules are designed to put money in their coffers and not ours. The rules they live by *accelerate* wealth, which is the exact opposite of what they tell consumers (you and me) to do: *accumulate* wealth. Hence, the money rains and flows into their accounts while it drips or dribbles into ours. Thus, the fight for our money is ongoing, every day of our lives.

RAINMAKER INTERACTION

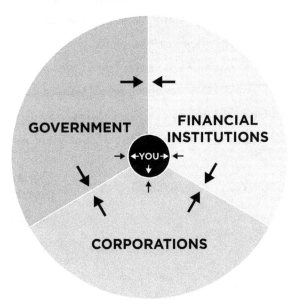

Figure 1.1

- Finite resources in our world
- The three rainmakers are constantly fighting for our money
- Rules change. Laws and new products are created to get more of our money

Today, most dentists who want to build wealth are unknowingly following the path of accumulating and compounding rather than accelerating their money. To find dentists who are accelerating their money is as rare as seeing an albino alligator. The three rainmakers, however, follow the wealth-building acceleration principle by keeping their money in motion. Again, they do the exact opposite of what they advise you and me to do. This is what drives their success and why they have the biggest and tallest buildings in every city across America.

The rainmakers are very skilled at separating you and me from our money. They employ many tactics to do this and frequently accomplish it without their actions being given a second thought by consumers. For example, the government uses different forms of taxation (see Figure 1.2) from the federal, state, and local level to reduce or influence our ability to succeed financially. An IRS auditor once said, "The trick is to stop thinking of it as 'your' money."

GOVERNMENT	CORPORATIONS	FINANCIAL INSTITUTIONS
Federal Taxes	Inflation	Investment Fees
State Taxes	Technological Change	Advisor Fees
Local Taxes	Style Changes	Inefficient Advice
Real Estate Taxes	Planned Obsolescence	Loan Interest
Sales Taxes	Advertising	Commissions
Capital Gains Taxes	False Advertising	Premiums
Estate Taxes	Quality Shrinkage	Market Losses
Licensing Fees	Quantity Shrinkage	Market Volatility
Gov't Student Loans	Service & Repair Fees	Penalties

Ways That the Rainmakers Take Our Money

Figure 1.2

Financial institutions grab our money through fees, commissions, bad advice, and scams. Corporations produce products with built-in planned obsolescence, requiring them to be replaced sooner than should be necessary, or they simply tweak the technology of an existing product and promote the new product as something you can't live without. The ongoing unveiling of the newest smartphone is a great example of this.

Finally, an underlying result of the rainmakers' quest for our money is the introduction of inflation into our lives. Inflation is a stealth tax that erodes a huge amount of our wealth over our lifetime. Many times, the impact of inflation is not fully understood until the consumer is in retirement and on a fixed income.

● ● ● ● ● ●

Inflation is when you pay fifteen dollars for the ten-dollar haircut you used to get for five dollars when you had hair.

—SAM EWING

● ● ● ● ● ●

All rainmakers have their own, individual game plan. The government is starving for taxes that keep it running. Corporations are hungry to sell products to satisfy shareholders. Financial institutions are fighting for the control of large blocks of our money, whether it is in the form of bank deposits, investments, or the sale of insurance products. These deposits all generate massive income in fees for the financial institutions. Yet, there are also times when the rainmakers work together.

A retirement plan is a perfect example of how financial institutions and the government work together to control huge monetary assets. First, the financial institution creates the mind-set that you must have a retirement account if you are ever going to retire, which is actually not true. This is promulgated by the accountants and advisors who share this same belief. As a result, you are convinced to contribute money to a retirement savings plan held at a financial institution.

Typically, the financial institution will get your money on an ongoing basis through weekly or biweekly payroll deductions. Once the financial institution has your money in hand, your money is, essentially, in jail, due to government rules that discourage you from withdrawing these funds prior to the age (as of today) of fifty-nine and a half. This restriction is a huge win for financial institutions as they get to control large blocks of money for a long period of time and collect their fees. If you withdraw your money prior to age fifty-nine and a half you will pay a 10 percent IRS penalty. Therefore, it is very expensive to get that money out of jail before you are fifty-nine and a half. The government is the entity that makes the rules on age of distribution, the type of taxes that need to be paid, penalties, and many other rules.

Now, when you get to retirement age, the rainmakers still want to retain control of your money. At that time, the financial institutions and traditional advisors will tell you that if you withdraw money from your retirement plan you will pay taxes on it, which is true. If you would like to avoid these taxes, though, the financial institutions and traditional advisors have a solution: you can simply defer distributions from this account until age seventy and a half. However, at that point, the government is going to *force* you to start taking withdrawals from your retirement plan through the required minimum distribution (RMD) provision. At this point, the government wants to start collecting on the account holder's deferred tax bill. The adoption of an RMD-only withdrawal strategy for retirement funds allows the financial institutions to hang on to your money and continue to collect ongoing fees for assets under their management.

The worst part of this whole situation is that the owners of the retirement plan end up getting little enjoyment from their retirement assets. The RMD distribution may minimize taxes, but at what expense to the retirees? They are now living on a minimum versus a maximum income distribution, all for the sake of further delaying a tax. Isn't the purpose of funding your retirement plan to fully enjoy it in the future? If so, you should be taking *maximum* distributions out of your retirement plan and not minimum distributions!

● ● ● ● ● ● ● ● ● ● ● ● ● ● ● ● ● ●

Tim

I graduated from college in 1984 and went to work for a big-eight public accounting firm. A month after starting, the senior partner called a meeting to introduce us to the new retirement plan that everybody was going to love. It was called a 401(k), which would replace the firm's long-standing defined benefit plan. As some of you may already know, a defined benefit plan is funded 100 percent by the company, which is great for the employee. A 401(k) plan, on the other hand, is, by and large, funded 100 percent by the employee, which is not great. This was the beginning of a huge shift that was taking place in corporations all over America at the time. Pensions were slowly being phased out and replaced by 401(k) plans. This shift was not advantageous to the consumers as they now became largely responsible for the funding of their own retirement.

The 401(k)'s selling point to me was the firm's matching contribution. If I were willing to contribute at least 3 percent, the firm would fully match the 3 percent contribution. With this in mind, right out of the gate, I started contributing 10 percent to the plan. Now in 1984, coming out of school as a certified public accountant, I made a whopping $18,000 a year. What tax bracket do you think I was in at that time? It was 10 percent, or the lowest bracket. It was nothing! Essentially, I deferred the 10 percent tax I would have paid on my money by putting my money into a retirement plan. If I were to retire today, those initial contributions that would otherwise have been taxed at 10 percent would now be taxed at the highest income tax bracket.

So who won that game? It wasn't me. In reality, it was the three rainmakers consisting of the government, corporations, and financial institutions. It's almost as if they colluded with one another at the expense of the consumer—or dentist.

• • • • • • • • • • • • • • • • • • • •

401(k)s were promoted to employees as a wonderful retirement option. In reality, the introduction of the 401(k) plan shifted not only the bulk of the funding but also all of the market risk away from the corporations to the individual. Financial institutions were thrilled with the restrictive laws imposed on the 401(k) plans, which prevented individuals from removing funds from their plans prior to age fifty-nine and a half, without incurring an early withdrawal penalty from the IRS. As a result, this one law alone has locked up billions of dollars in invested funds with the financial institutions that are collecting advisory and management fees. The fees collected each year are like a huge annuity to the financial institutions whether the market does well or not.

Finally, those who have a retirement plan such as a 401(k) plan are in a one-sided partnership with the government in that the government makes all of the rules and laws regarding a 401(k) plan. The government tells us how much we can contribute to the plan, at what age we can take funds out of the plan, and how much we will, ultimately, pay in taxes. Also, keep in mind that all long-term capital gains in a retirement plan are taxed as ordinary income and not as capital gains. Tax rates on ordinary income can be as high as 37 percent versus a capital gains rate as low as 15 percent—if the funds were held in an after-tax investment account. For this one fact alone, the difference in potential tax revenues between ordinary and capital gains taxes to the government will be significant over time. We also must take into consideration that tax rates may very well increase over time, which will benefit the government even more. The 401(k) plan and everything that goes along with it is a prime example of how all three rainmakers benefit at the expense of the consumer.

There was a time when you could withdraw your retirement funds at any age, without penalty. Then the government, due to intense lobbying from the financial institutions, put in place restrictive regulations that included penalties for withdrawing money from a retirement account before age fifty-nine and a half. The government can regulate or deregulate, and it can do this in favor or not in favor of the consumer. Therefore, we must be cognizant that laws governing retirement plans can and will change in the future, whether it is for the advantage or disadvantage of the consumer.

If the rainmakers are always moving money under their control for their benefit, then doesn't it make sense that your money should always be in motion too? Anything in life that sits in one place too long will go stale or break down. In other words, it stagnates! Whether it is your health or your money, you need to keep it moving.

Often, dentists resist the concept of money in motion. What they really want is to put their money somewhere and not have to think about it again. They just want to make a money decision and be done with it. Since compound interest is believed to be a good thing in the traditional world of finance, they think they are okay, when in reality their money is rotting right before their eyes.

Why? It's due to the fact that dentists, and the general public, have been directed by financial institutions, accountants, family members, and others to think this way. When we let our money stagnate with the financial institutions, the financial institutions, along with the advisors, are collecting a fee on that invested money. They make money whether your account balance is going up or down. Why would the financial institutions and their many advisors want to give up managing trillions of dollars when they collect a fee that can be 1 percent or higher each and every year?

Over time, dentists will purchase many different insurance and financial products. These purchases are often made one at a time, with different advisors or agents, at different times in a dentist's life. Once the decision about the purchase is made, it is never revisited. This creates a lot disorganization. Everyone knows that disorganization is never good and results in extreme inefficiency when it comes to building wealth. This assortment of unorganized financial products is like your kitchen junk drawer in that you know what is in the drawer, but it takes a while to find what you want.

In this personal financial junk drawer, nothing is coordinated or integrated. Decisions that were made at different points in life are now oftentimes working against each other—very inefficient. This becomes stressful for dentists, but they don't know how to fix it, and so avoid the issue. They don't want to deal with it until introduced to our Financial Treatment Plan.

When you have a Financial Treatment Plan, the disorganization and confusion disappears. Everything is put in its appropriate place and every decision is evaluated from a macroeconomic standpoint. This alone brings tremendous peace of mind to dentists in their personal financial lives. A Financial Treatment Plan allows them to actually visualize and understand their finances and not fear them. It gets them excited to have a better understanding of how their money works and allows them to be proactive with their financial decisions rather than reactive.

When it comes to retirement planning, dentists are taught to max out their retirement contributions but are not taught how to maximize other aspects of their financial lives. If they are only accumulating money, a lot of other people (e.g., financial institutions and advisors) benefit from such a decision without the dentists even knowing it.

That problem is further compounded because there is usually no discussion about an exit or distribution strategy for retirement. Without this discussion, as we said earlier, most retired dentists are leading quiet lives of economic desperation. This is due to the blind focus they placed on only accumulating assets during their working years, with little or no conversation regarding distribution in retirement. They may still be living in the same house and driving the same car (although it is a few years older), but things are tight—and that's just unnecessary.

● ● ● ● ● ● ● ● ● ● ● ● ● ● ● ● ● ● ●

Tim

Various financial magazines will tell you that you only need 60–70 percent of your income in retirement. Better yet, you can have a successful retirement in Costa Rica because the cost of living is so cheap there, or you can move to a US state with no state income tax. The articles will sing the praises of the expat life or living in a state with no state income tax, and they may be right. Your cost of living and taxes may be less as a result of these choices, but you may retire without having family, friends, and everything you know around you. What kind of life is that? That doesn't sound like happiness. Who wants to live out retirement only seeing kids and grandkids once a year? Is that the lasting memory you want to have of them? Living in a foreign country or a tax-free state may be great, if done because you choose to live that way, and not because you have to!

● ● ● ● ● ● ● ● ● ● ● ● ● ● ● ● ● ● ●

We can be angry about the control the rainmakers have over our money, or we can learn from their actions. We have established that financial institutions work on the principle of keeping money in motion, or the velocity of money principle, so let's look at an example. We open a bank account where we make ongoing deposits. Depending on the type of account, the bank may pay us a small amount of interest. Once the bank has our money on deposit, does it just sit on it? The answer is a resounding *no.* The bank will take our money, as well as that of other bank depositors, and use it to its benefit. The bank doesn't sit on the money, as it tells us to do. Instead, it turns around and makes a loan to another individual. Perhaps it's a car loan for one person, and a mortgage loan for somebody else. Then it makes a loan to a college student. As the loan payments come back into the bank, what does the bank do? It lends that money again. The Federal Reserve says that every dollar that moves through a banking institution can turn over as many as fifty-five times each year, or about once a week.[5] But not for you.

Conventional thinking will have you believe that when the bank charges you 4 percent for a car loan and you're earning 1 percent on your savings account at the bank, that bank is only making 3 percent on this transaction. In reality, however, that 3 percent spread represents a 300 percent profit for the bank. As previously discussed, the bank will repeat the transaction, creating new loans with your money many times over during the course of the year. Is it any wonder that banks have some of the largest buildings in every city across the world? This is an example of velocity of money at its finest.

● ● ● ● ● ● ● ● ● ● ● ● ● ● ● ● ●

Mart

Remember the 1960s television show *The Beverly Hillbillies*? In one episode, Jed Clampett, the millionaire hillbilly, visits Mr. Drysdale, the president of the bank. Jed asks to see his money. He wants Mr. Drysdale to show him his million dollars. Jed was assuming that there was a stack of bills sitting in the bank's vault that was his money. Of course, even then, Jed's money was moving all over the

---

5   Gottfried Leibbrandt, "How fast is that buck?" The SWIFT Institute, July 23, 2012, https://swiftinstitute.org/2012/07/how-fast-is-that-buck.

place. So, Mr. Drysdale ends up showing him a picture of a million dollars just to appease him. Of course, the money pictured wasn't really Jed's money, as banks *do not* let the money sit and stagnate.

• • • • • • • • • • • • • • • • • • • •

Traditionally, if we have money in a bank or an investment account, as it earns interest, dividends, and capital gains, we have been taught to compound the earnings right back into the account. If we do that, we lose control of the asset because we have just allowed those earnings to compound back into the account and go stale. Why not take our interest, dividends, and capital gains and move those earnings to some other part of our Financial Treatment Plan and make another use of that dollar. Each time we make another use of a dollar we gain increased benefits and additional rates of return. We will actually verify this money strategy in our "Money Myths Debunked" chapter (chapter 4) when we discuss an alternative to compounding interest.

Keeping money in motion is all about getting multiple uses out of every dollar and not letting any dollar die by sitting too long in one spot in the Financial Treatment Plan. Allowing your money to sit in one place too long is like having a blood clot in the body that prevents the blood from flowing through your organs! Blood clots cause heart attacks and strokes. If you have stale or stagnant money in your personal finances, you are placing your present and future financial situation on life support! This is one of the many reasons why the average dentist retires with a 50 percent pay cut in retirement.

Think of it as a chess game. Every chess piece has different strengths and powers, just as every financial product has advantages and disadvantages. The objective of chess is to get to checkmate in the shortest number of moves possible in order to win the match. No single move or chess piece will win the game. Rather, games are won through a series of moves that strategically position many chess pieces in order to secure a victory. As an example, the queen is the most powerful chess piece on the board. However, if that is all you have on the board, you will not win the game. The game of finance is much like chess in that you will need multiple financial products that are strategically placed and in constant motion. It is this type of game play that will help you achieve your full wealth potential and avoid a pay cut in retirement.

Instead of being taught the money chess game, dentists have been taught to put their money in one place and let it sit, as, for example, in a retirement plan. In doing so, they are handcuffing their money, because once it goes into that retirement plan, it is locked up until the dentists are fifty-nine and a half years of age. Once that dollar goes in, they're never going to get another use out of it throughout their accumulation period. This is very inefficient. To be clear, though, we are not saying that retirement plans are bad. Instead, we are saying that you need to understand the ramifications of putting money into that type of account as a first move of your money.

Also, dentists are taught to focus on achieving high returns in their investments, which, oftentimes, causes them to chase a rate of return to their detriment. Contrary to the popular opinion of investment advisors, the rate of return is not nearly as important as you think. Why? Because the existence of wealth-eroding factors in a Financial Treatment Plan will have a far bigger impact than a rate of return will ever have on your wealth. These wealth-eroding factors attack your money twenty-four hours a day, seven days a week, each and every year of your life. The ramifications of taxes and inflation are two of the better-known wealth-eroding factors that people face daily. Most people already understand how these factors negatively affect their wealth, but there are a number of other factors that also impact wealth.

In fact, upward of 12 percent of your money is being eroded away on a yearly basis due to taxes, inflation, planned obsolescence, technological change, and unexpected life events. This means you have to save at least 12 percent each year just to overcome these wealth-eroding factors alone. In order to outpace these basic effects of wealth erosion, you must establish the discipline of saving a minimum of 15 percent of your income each year. If you do not save at this rate, then you are going backward.

The object of keeping your money in motion is to pick up individual rates of return and increased benefits each time you turn, or move, the money. With each move you may get 5 percent here, 5 percent there and 5 percent over there. Add those up and you're getting a 15 percent rate of return with less risk and more benefit. Again, this velocity of money principle will be highlighted in the compound interest example discussed in chapter 4, "Money Myths Debunked." Investors in this day and age find a 5 percent rate of return decent, but 5 percent taken multiple times with increased benefits is a home-run investment.

We hear the question all the time: What rate of return are your investments getting? If this is your primary concern, I can share with you that you're asking the wrong question. Your question should be, How am I going to overcome the wealth eroders of life and do so with less risk? If you *only* focused on overcoming wealth-eroding factors, you would achieve success beyond your wildest dreams.

Because dentists are smart, some dentists believe they can manage their own money. After all, there's a lot of financial information out in the media today to help do-it-yourselfers make financial decisions. For example, at Fidelity.com, you can read that if you have eight times your salary saved by age sixty, you are on the right track. So, let's put some numbers to this advice and assume you are making $500,000 a year, prior to retirement. According to this advice you would then only need $4,000,000 of saved assets when you retire. Again, using the traditional world's advice for retirement income planning, you would then take a 3 percent safe withdrawal from these assets for an annual retirement income of $120,000. If you are a do-it-yourselfer and follow this advice, you will set yourself up to take about a 75 percent pay cut in retirement! This is one of the reasons why we are adamant that do-it-yourselfers will struggle to reach their full wealth potential.

You can go online and find different financial calculators for retirement. With each one, you can input how much money will be saved on an annual basis, your expected rate of return, and the number of years you have before you retire. Click the magic button and you are told how much money you will have when you retire. If this final retirement sum is not enough, you have one of two choices: either save more money or chase a higher rate of return. If you can't save more money, you then simply plug in a higher rate of return until you get the result you want, as though you are guaranteed to realize the higher rate of return. Even if this is guaranteed, you have now assumed much more risk and volatility in your planning, but you feel better because you are now on track for retirement.

This is not retirement planning! It's just playing math games with numbers until you get a result you like. It is the proverbial massaging of the numbers for financial comfort. Online calculators are a detriment to your long-term financial health. They often provide a false sense of security, indicating that your financial plan is on track for success. Unfortunately, they are an essential planning tool for the do-it-yourselfer.

If you look at truly successful people, whether they are in business, sports, or entertainment, almost every one of them has a coach. For example, a golfer may have several coaches: a swing coach, a physical trainer, and a putting instructor. It's possible there might even be a sports psychologist on board to help the golfer deal with the mental aspects of the game.

Why is it, then, that dentists fight the idea of having a financial coach to help them navigate the confusing world of personal finance?

Too often, the reason dentists are disappointed with their financial portfolios is because their advisors have only focused these portfolios on accumulating assets that are driven by a rate of return. Focusing on the accumulation of assets leads to frustration as markets fluctuate and returns are not what were expected. As a result, many dentists will make the decision to just do it themselves. Financial success, however, is not a rate of return equation. Rate of return is only *part* of the puzzle.

Financial success is having the maximum benefits from a maximum money supply at all times in your life. This is the foundation for what creates enjoyment in dentists' lives, ultimately a retirement where they do not take pay cuts and have guarantees built in to their retirement incomes. The guarantees are what provide immense peace of mind to dentists in retirement, because no matter what happens, they know with certainty that they will never run out of money.

As we have discussed, the rainmakers are fighting for your money, so you need to know how to counterpunch and not sit back and let your wealth be eroded away. The great philosopher Mike Tyson once said, "Everyone has a plan until they get punched in the mouth!" By understanding that the rules the rainmakers follow are different from the rules they promote for you and me as consumers, you will have significantly more wealth than the average dentist and avoid being knocked out financially. It is the old saying: if you can't beat them, join them.

One of our many objectives is to help you discover how to live by the same rules as the rainmakers. It is our hope that we will expose you to eye-opening information when it comes to your personal finances and get you excited about a macroeconomic model for your money. Let's start by looking at the big money picture.

Chapter 2

THE BIG MONEY PICTURE

• • •

May you find INSPIRATION in the big picture,
but may you find LOVE in the details.

—ADRIENNE MALOOF

t has been reported that six in ten baby boomers feared running out of money before they died more than death itself.[6] Even though dentists make a lot of money during their working years, they are no different in regard to their anxieties. They, too, fear running out of money. Developing strategies to position dentists to hold multiple income streams in retirement creates a bulletproof plan, so that no matter what happens, they *can't* run out of money. This takes that fear off the table!

According to the IRS, multimillionaires will have, on average, seven different sources of income in retirement. Unfortunately, the majority of dentists who retire will only have three to four income streams. If you reduce the stress brought on by fear, your health will

---

6   Catey Hill, "Older people fear this more than death," MarketWatch, July 21, 2016, https://www.marketwatch.com/story/older-people-fear-this-more-than-death-2016-07-18.

most likely improve. You're better psychologically and physically. You may even live longer. Peace of mind is priceless.

To help our clients gain that peace of mind, we begin by looking at what we call the big picture. In the big money picture, there are three wealth-building phases: accumulation, distribution, and preservation, all of which are supported by a *wrapper*. The traditional financial world looks at the three phases of wealth building as if they occur in a linear pattern: one after the other. The reality is that every financial decision a person makes, whether that person is young or old, can and does have an impact on at least two if not all three phases of wealth building *simultaneously*. This is critically important to understand. Financial decisions are dynamic. A decision regarding accumulation doesn't just affect the accumulation of your wealth; it also affects the distribution and preservation of your money at the same time. That is one of the big disconnects between what we do as macroadvisors, and what traditional microfinancial advisors do. We make sure we account for each of these phases in every decision that our dental clients make.

The three wealth phases—accumulation, distribution, and preservation—have historically been presented to us as individual phases we encounter, based on age. The accumulation phase, which is all about accruing or growing wealth, is normally thought to be the period of time during our working career leading to retirement. Frequently, in the traditional world of finance, we are led to believe that the accumulation phase stops at retirement. Why can't the accumulation phase continue throughout our entire lifetime? Accomplishing lifelong accumulation would be the ideal and something that every dentist would want.

In the traditional world of finance, the wealth distribution phase is thought to cover the period of twenty to thirty years called retirement. We believe the time horizon of this wealth phase is actually much longer, starting early in dentists' careers and continuing until their death. This is due to our definition of wealth distribution, which defines this phase as the spending and enjoyment of personal assets both today and in the future without the fear of ever running out of money.

In other words, how do you position yourself to have maximum retirement income with guarantees in the future and still enjoy life to the fullest today? This could mean owning a second home at the lake or on the beach now rather than later. Wouldn't you want to do this and more while working and know with certainty that your retirement is secure? Having a retirement plan with no distribution strategy to fully enjoy your earnings is not retirement planning. Discussions about your wealth distribution strategies and desires should start during your working years and continue throughout your lifetime. As a matter of fact, an important question that you should ask and answer prior to making any investment is, How am I going to get this money out in the future to enjoy?

The preservation phase, in the traditional world, represents the time at the end of your life. This is a time when assets are hopefully passed on intact to loved ones or charity. Unfortunately, due to ineffective planning throughout a dentist's life, more of a dentist's wealth is passed on to the government in the form of unnecessary taxes, and to corporations (e.g., long-term-care facilities), financial institutions, and lastly, other wealthy people (e.g., fire/estate, sales). Again, just like the previous two wealth phases, accumulation and distribution, the preservation phase should be addressed and considered with each financial decision during a dentist's lifetime.

Traditional financial planners look at each of these three phases as singular phases of life. Yet, every decision has lasting effects that impact all three phases, regardless of age. This is why it is so important to know the impact on each wealth phase—accumulation, distribution, and preservation—when making financial decisions. Again, this is another reason why a macroeconomic model, such as the Financial Treatment Plan, is so important to financial well-being.

For example, you can make a solid accumulation decision, such as funding a retirement plan, and pick up some tax advantages by doing so. You will get a pretax deduction on the contribution and your growth on the investment is tax deferred, both good things. But too often there is no thought given to how you are going to get that money out of the retirement plan. If you wait until retirement to make that distribution decision, by default you have put shackles on how much you will be able to actually enjoy your wealth in your later years. Remember the 50 percent pay-cut discussion? Since you did not make an exit strategy ahead of time, you will be left with significantly less income in retirement—in the neighborhood of a 50 percent loss of income for the average dentist!

Understanding how the different phases interact with each other is essential, but it also important to have wealth objectives that are coordinated with each of the phases. We call this a financial mission statement. Most dentists will have a mission statement for their practice but never consider having one for their personal finances. A mission statement is nothing more than a statement of purpose. When a dentist has a financial mission statement for building wealth, financial decisions can be made with confidence if the money decisions align with the mission's stated purpose. The following four objectives make up the financial mission statement. We use these as a framework to overcome the emotions and opinions that come with every financial decision. These objectives/mission statement are the first step in peace of mind planning.

FIRST OBJECTIVE: BUILD WEALTH EFFICIENTLY WITH LESS RISK

Our first objective is to help dentists maximize the building of their wealth in the most efficient manner possible without increasing risk. Again, that is counterintuitive to the traditional world of finance because we have all been led to believe that if we want more wealth, we have to take more risk and chase a higher rate of return. If a plan is efficient, an overall high rate of return will be achieved in the macroeconomic model with less risk. Understanding the strategy behind financial products and how to properly use them in combination with one another as part of your Financial Treatment Plan drives efficiency. Embracing this philosophy will create additional wealth for you by making use of the same dollars in your present financial plan but not taking additional risk.

In order to increase efficiency, you need to keep your money in motion, as the rainmakers do. By doing so, you can use the same inputs that you are already utilizing and not change your present lifestyle. Your standard of living stays the same. We decrease the waste and offset some of the eroding factors, such as taxes and inflation. By reengineering the flow of these dollars, you will have an increased money supply and gain additional benefits. This is the real differentiator that will take you to that next level of wealth creation. Always remember that the longer your money stagnates (by sitting in one place), the more you are reducing the overall efficiency of your plan. You have to keep your money moving!

A perfect financial plan is a series of one-year perfect plans that need to be fine-tuned annually. Think of it as being like car maintenance. If you take care of your car, it will last longer. On the other hand, if you don't take care of your car—by skipping a tune-up or maybe changing your oil less frequently than recommended—then your car is going to deteriorate much faster than it would on a regular maintenance schedule.

The efficient approach is to have the car serviced periodically: oil change, spark plugs, tire rotation, fluid check, and so on. After servicing the car, you get the same car back, but it operates more efficiently. Simple maintenance of a car allows it to perform better and last longer. We want to do the same with your money from an efficiency standpoint so that the same dollars give you greater financial output now and in the long run.

The concept of buying a car and driving it for five years with no regular maintenance is similar to the traditional world's approach to your financial life. Within the dental world, the conventional wisdom is to maximize your qualified retirement plan contributions through a 401(k)/profit-sharing plan. Then, if you are contributing the maximum and you still have excess funds to save, your advisor may tell you to add a cash balance plan. Depending on how the cash balance plan is structured you may be able to contribute upward of another couple hundred thousand dollars or more. Now your money just sits there in a retirement investment account with occasional asset allocation changes and waits for you to retire. In other words, it stagnates! You think you're doing the right thing, but the truth is that a retirement plan by itself will result in very few retirement income options. It is the old proverbial adage of putting all your eggs in one basket. Very inefficient!

Another traditional inefficient approach is dollar cost averaging (DCA) into after-tax plans. DCA is an investment technique that involves buying a fixed dollar amount of a particular investment on a regular schedule, regardless of the share price. This is all about accumulating assets with no regard to what the exit or distribution strategy will be. Nor are the many eroding factors involved considered.

Nobody is talking to you about the negative effects that go along with these traditional decisions. The reality is that every financial decision you make will have negative as well as positive effects. There is no one perfect product. If there were, we'd all buy it and we would all be wealthy. The key is being as efficient as possible in accentuating the positive effects and mitigating the negative ones.

In order to be successful in your financial life, you must have balance. If you place too much weight on any one area of your financial life—whether it is in a retirement plan, investments, real estate, or life insurance—at the expense of the other areas, you are susceptible to future problems. You need to have balance. Having balance always results in less risk in your financial life.

Traditionally, risk is associated with a higher rate of return, which is just *one* of many factors that will determine your eventual wealth. Those who focus *only* on a rate of return to drive the success of their financial plan will be disappointed at some point due to their heavy reliance on market results. As we all know, the stock market cannot be controlled. The market will go up and it will go down; we never know how to time it effectively. Unknowns, such as flying a plane into the World Trade Center or an interest rate adjustment by the Federal Reserve will impact the stock market. We cannot change that.

Another factor that impacts your wealth-building capability is your annual savings rate. If you are not disciplined and saving at least 15 percent each year, it doesn't matter if you get a 20 percent rate of return on your money. A small savings amount, despite a high rate of return, still does not end up being that much. The most important factor in wealth building is the ability to save as much money as you can. If you can't save, it will be almost impossible to achieve financial success regardless of the rate of return earned. You will also work much longer than you want to.

Many times, when we work with dentists, they talk about their investment successes but rarely mention their investment losses. Yet, 46 percent of orthodontists felt that money lost due to investments was a barrier to being financially prepared for retirement.[7] The reality is that you will experience both successes and failures in your financial life. As such, for financial success to occur you must maximize the wins and minimizing the losses. If you earn 10 percent on one investment and take a loss in another investment, this is not a 10 percent win. Your net gain or loss is a combination of the two investment results. Therefore, the rate of return on any one investment does not determine your financial state. As much as your present advisors may tell you that investment rate of return is important, it is just another part of your financial equation.

When people chase the rate of return, they end up shooting themselves in the foot because they are focused solely on what the market is doing or not doing. For example, as we write this book, we have had an incredible bull run in the markets, but at some point in the future, there will be a market correction. When that occurs, panic for some will set in, especially for those who have small cash positions for liquidity. Dentists in this situation are caught in the position of having to get out of the market because they don't have the cash reserves to stomach a big loss. As the well-respected investor Larry Swedroe (director of research, BAM Alliance) said, "I've yet to meet a stomach that makes good decisions."

Dentists who are caught in this situation and sell in a low market often end up with their money on the sidelines in a money market account. They often have no idea of when to reinvest in the market. This unknown can cost them a ton of money. No one has a crystal

---

7   Jeremiah Sturgill and Jae Park, "Changes in Orthodontists' Retirement Planning and Practice Operations Due to the Recent Recession."

ball forecasting the right moment to get back into the investing game. What's going to be your cue? When the market goes down? If yes, how far does the market need to go down before you get back in? And how much are you going to reinvest?

When you do make the decision to get back in the market, you may buy back in at a higher position than you initially sold. If that is the case, you missed out on some gains by delaying your reentry into the market. This is why chasing a rate of return without having a real investment strategy for your plan is not likely to be a successful journey. It is truly an exercise in futility, yet, everyone does it, and so it must be correct, right? Wrong!

A well-respected investment study on market returns was conducted by Dalbar. The table on the next page shows that the S&P 500 has delivered a market rate of return of 5.62 percent over the past twenty years. The average investor over that same time period only received a return of 3.88 percent. This represents a 31 percent difference between what the S&P 500 actually delivered in the market versus what the average investor received. For many, this will translate into hundreds of thousands—if not millions—of dollars of lost wealth. In this case, the 1.74 percent difference in rate of return that was lost is due primarily to the emotions experienced by investors who didn't have a strategic way of looking at their investments.

WHY DO ACTIVE INVESTORS FAIL?

	ANNUALIZED RETURN
S&P 500 Index	5.62%
Average Equity Fund Investor	3.88%
Bloomberg Barclays Aggregate Bond Index	5.29%
Average Fixed Income Fund Investor	0.48%
Average Equity Fund Investor Holding Period	3.5 Years

Source: "DALBAR 2018 QAIB—Quantitative Analysis of Investor Behavior, covering the period of January 1, 1997 through December 31, 2016," DALBAR, https://svwealth.com/wp-content/uploads/2018/04/dalbar_study.pdf.[8]

Table 2.1

Keep in mind that any market rate of return presented to you is either based on a projection of anticipated future results or past performance. Nobody knows what the future holds, and by no means is this projection a guarantee of what you will actually receive.

---

8   Dalbar is the financial community's leading independent expert in evaluating, auditing, and rating business practices, customer performance, product quality, and service. Launched in 1976, Dalbar has earned recognition for consistent and unbiased evaluations of investment companies, registered investment advisers, insurance companies, broker/dealers, retirement plan providers and financial professionals. (Dalbar.com)

Also, when evaluating the merits of a financial decision, you must consider the other variables or benefits that result from that decision, such as whether there are tax ramifications. Are you picking up a disability benefit? Is there a premature death benefit or better yet a living benefit? Will you receive a tax deduction, a tax deferral, or tax-free access on your funds? Are the funds liquid or are they locked up? Can you get to them prior to fifty-nine and a half? In other words, if you want to make good financial decisions, you must account for all of the advantages and disadvantages surrounding that decision and not just consider the potential rate of return.

An efficient Financial Treatment Plan is judged by the sum of all of its parts. It is not just a rate of return or any one variable or benefit resulting from a financial decision that makes a plan great. Instead, it is all of these things that allow us to create wealth efficiently and with less risk.

SECOND OBJECTIVE: SPEND *AND* ENJOY YOUR WEALTH WITHOUT THE FEAR OF RUNNING OUT OF MONEY

Our second objective deals with the distribution phase of wealth enhancement. A properly designed distribution phase allows dentists to have their cake and eat it too. This powerful objective is aimed at allowing our clients to be able to fully spend and enjoy their wealth today, as well as in the future, *without* the fear of running out of funds.

In the traditional world of financial planning, the distribution phase of life is concentrated on retirement. Traditional planners of all types typically tell you that you get to enjoy your money after you retire. Your career as a dentist has spanned thirty to forty years, during which time you have hopefully acquired some wealth. Did you work and set money aside to enjoy in retirement only? We hope not, for it's possible that an accident or illness may prevent you from ever seeing retirement. Mart's father passed away at the age of sixty-five after working for more than thirty years for IBM. Did he get to enjoy his retirement? The answer is an emphatic no! We want our clients to have the freedom as well as the permission to spend and enjoy their wealth both today and in the future.

For instance, if you want to own a second home, be it on the lake, the beach, or in the mountains, why wait until you retire? Why not make that purchase when your kids are young and still want to spend time with you? That's the time to create family memories. Purchasing a second home when our children were young is one of the best things we have done for our families. What do you think the rate of return has been on those investments? The rate of return from enjoyment has been infinite!

The traditional financial world scares you by saying that if you are not putting money away through investments, you will not have enough money in the future for your retirement. That's what we call a scarcity mentality. Remember traditional planners live in a world of assets under management. Their advice preys on fear and guilt. They also benefit from a client mind-set of maintaining the status quo or minimal change. In the end, advisors manage a lot of money in retirement accounts, while dentists receive little enjoyment during their working years from that same money.

Our mind-set works in total opposition to the strategies of traditional planners. We want to help you develop a financial life that allows you to fully enjoy your money when you are young and healthy, and at the same time gets you to the retirement stage with full income replacement. Better yet, we want your retirement income to have guarantees built in that ensure your money will never run out.

Saving, investing, and spending are not mutually exclusive things. Almost every dentist we meet is making maximum contributions to a qualified plan. Today (2019), dentists under the age of fifty can contribute a maximum of $56,000 a year to their 401(k), safe-harbor, and profit-sharing plan. If the dentists are fifty or older, they can contribute a maximum of $62,000 to these plans. That's a lot of money. Again, once it goes into the retirement plan, it is in prison. Dentists can't access it prior to age fifty-nine and a half without paying hefty penalties or dealing with a convoluted process. The retirement plan is not liquid, and is solely dependent upon what the market does or does not do. Even worse, dentists are getting only one use out of that money over many years, and that is never good.

Instead of throwing all of your money into a retirement plan, why not max out the employee and safe harbor contributions of $19,000 and $11,200, respectively. The retirement plan is now funded with $30,200 for the year. That leaves $25,800 that would have gone into profit sharing if you had elected to fund the plan. In addition, if you suspend your profit-sharing-plan contribution, you may save another $6,000 to $8,000 that would have gone to other employees. You now have up to $33,800 that you can take as a distribution. Of course, taxes must be paid on this amount, but this sum could go a long way in supporting a mortgage on a second home.

For the same dollars, you now have a retirement plan *and* a second home to enjoy. If the second home is located in a vacation destination area, perhaps it could be rented out when you are not using it, which creates another income stream. It really is like having your cake and eating it too. You have your retirement plan for later, and a second home to enjoy today. You also may have created an income-producing asset, and guess what? Real estate in areas where second homes are located tend to appreciate over time. Down the road, if you elect to sell the second home, the appreciation is treated as a capital gain, which is taxed at 15–20 percent today. This is opposed to all gains in a retirement plan that are taxed at the highest ordinary income tax bracket that you fall into at the time of withdrawal. Today that rate could be as high as 37 percent. This is a great example of a win-win strategy where the two objectives of investing in a retirement plan and enjoying your earnings today were addressed with the same money.

Everyone loves this objective because dentists can have their cake and eat it too. We believe that people don't make money to hoard it, but to enjoy it! With that in mind, there needs to be built-in strategies to overcome the greatest fear people face in retirement: running out of money. Therefore, guarantees are built in to the Financial Treatment Plan for ultimate peace of mind in retirement. Enjoy your cake!

THIRD OBJECTIVE: ENJOY YOUR WEALTH AND PASS ON THE REST

Our third objective deals with the preservation or conservation of your wealth. If we have followed the macrofinancial blueprint well and created maximum wealth in the Financial Treatment Plan over a lifetime, then there is going to be money left over for loved ones or charities in the future. At the end of your life, your money can only go to one of six places: the government, financial institutions, corporations, other wealthy people, your family, or charities.

Of those six, where do most dentists want to see their wealth go? The answer is, obviously, to family, charities, or both. The unfortunate thing is that due to improper planning, more wealth gets transferred to those first four groups than it does to family or charities. The takeaway is this: if you want your wealth to go to your family and/or charities, then you need to plan for that to happen.

Most dentists have a charitable intent. They would like to see some of their wealth go to charity, but for most, this does not happen, because they are afraid they won't have enough money to live on in retirement. They're not sure how long they're going to live, and many are not sure how to make a sizable charitable gift other than, maybe, a gift at death.

Often, dentists (including most advisors) don't understand the powerful charitable giving strategies that are available to them. The number-one form of charitable giving is writing a check and taking the deduction on your tax return that year. In doing so, you only get one benefit from that transaction, which is the tax deduction on the donation. Why not utilize a simple strategy that we call turbotithe. This straightforward strategy will be discussed in greater detail in chapter 8. It's like hitting a triple instead of a single in baseball.

The *most* powerful charitable strategy, however, is a planning strategy that encompasses a number of financial moves. First, it positions dentists to give to charity while not disinheriting loved ones or family members. Most importantly, dentists will receive increased retirement income over and above what they would have received if they had not given to charity. It is a triple win for the charity, the dentists' heirs, and the dentists, as donors. It is a unique strategy that gets everyone excited. More on this later in the book!

The triple win may seem counterintuitive to ordinary thinking, but it is possible. Everybody thinks that giving money away to a charity means having less in total assets. Thus, their income is reduced because the assets that were given to the charity are no longer producing income. If you simply write a check as a one-time donation, this is true. But if you have a strategic charitable plan, the act of giving can create income while you're alive and you will not disinherit the family.

We also believe that there is an enjoyment to giving to charity while you're alive rather than just designating assets to a charity after you die. When you arrange for your donations to be made after your death, you never get to see the benefits of your generosity. The best time to give to charity is when you are young because you will be able to see the benefits of your gift, which also include the fact that when you are more giving, you tend to be happier.

If the majority of dentists choose family and friends as their legacy choices, why does most of their money end up going to the first four groups?

If the estate is large enough, there could be estate taxes paid to the government unnecessarily. There can also be taxes paid upon death that could have been avoided with proper planning. Therefore, the government wins and you lose. Incurring significant long-term care expenses certainly makes corporations rich and depletes estates, which reduces the amount that can be passed on to family or charities. Without proper planning, the elderly can pass an extraordinary amount of wealth to a long-term-care facility at the end of their life. In a worst-case scenario, the house you thought you were going to leave to your kids ends up going to the state as reimbursement for Medicaid nursing home payments. Even if the house remains in the possession of your family, often the estate has, basically, been spent down to nothing because there was no long-term-care strategy in place. Therefore, the corporations win and you lose!

With inefficient products in place, financial institutions will continue to erode your wealth with high fees or low rates of return paid on your investments. Over an extended period of time this can reduce the amount of your estate and what you ultimately pass on to loved ones or charities when you die. Once again, financial institutions win and you lose!

Finally, other wealthy people can benefit from the fire sale of the possessions in your estate.

These are just some of the examples of what can happen when you have not properly planned in the preservation phase: Wealth is often lost, and families and charities are the biggest losers. The winners should be your family and your chosen charities, not the other groups!

FOURTH WEALTH OBJECTIVE: THE WRAPPER

Dentists love our first three wealth objectives aimed at creating maximum wealth without increased risk, being able to spend and enjoy their maximum wealth without the fear of running out of money in retirement, and then ensuring that their legacies go to family and charities. We've never had any dentists tell us that they don't want these objectives.

Our fourth objective, which we refer to as the wrapper, ties everything together. It is simply this: failure is not an option. In other words, you have to have contingency plans in place to offset all the various life events that can and do happen throughout our lifetime. Most financial plans are based on a best-case scenario, and if you draw that picture on a spreadsheet, it always looks good. They assume, for example, that dentists will always receive a consistent and high rate of return on their investments year in and year out; tax rates will never change; and dentists and their families will never encounter a health or family crisis that requires a monetary outlay to address the crisis. What about a disability, premature death, or some other career disruption that drains resources? You will be sadly disappointed at some point if your financial plan's success is contingent on a best-case scenario only.

The problem is that life happens. We all experience both good and bad life events. With that in mind we should build financial plans that will be successful under *all* circumstances. Failure cannot be an option! Financial Treatment Plans need to address all ways that failure can creep into the plan. When a Financial Treatment Plan is properly structured for success, there is no cost differential between having a financial plan that is built on the best-case scenario versus a plan that's built on the worst-case scenario. So if costs were the same, why wouldn't we want to have success ensured under the worst-case scenario since the best-case scenario never happens?

When a Financial Treatment Plan is built in this fashion and a worst-case scenario occurs, your plan is still going to be successful. Also, anything better than the worst-case scenario will be icing on the cake. Perhaps you will live a charmed life and never experience a negative life event. Keep in mind, however, that even one unforeseen event that is not planned for could bring down your financial house if your financial plan is only based on best-case scenarios.

• • • • • • • • • • • • • • • • • • • •

Mart

I had open-heart surgery at age forty-five due to an undiagnosed congenital heart valve defect. That's not a normal thing, right? You don't expect that. Nobody in their right mind would assume they would have open-heart surgery at age forty-five. When I was wheeled into the operating room, I was very aware that I might not make it out alive.

Thankfully, my Financial Treatment Plan was positioned in such a way that if anything had happened to me, I knew with 100 percent certainty that my wife and kids would be totally fine financially for the rest of their lives. Knowing this, I went into surgery with total peace of mind and less worry, which I believe helped lower my stress and improve my overall recovery process. Those are the plans we like to build for our clients.

• • • • • • • • • • • • • • • • • • • •

• • • • • • • • • • • • • • • • • • • •

Tim

Early in my career, during the decade of the 1990s, the stock market had one of its best runs ever. The annualized return in the S&P 500 for that decade was almost 18 percent. Then we had the dot-com bust followed by the September 11 terrorist attack, which dramatically impacted the markets from 2000 to 2002. For many invested in the market, this was a very unsettling time.

In late 2002, I was introduced to a dentist who had retired at the end of 1999 with over $4 million in his retirement plan. When this dentist initially retired, he thought he had more than enough money to live on. Then the market crashed. At the time I was introduced to the dentist, his original $4 million retirement account was now less than $2 million. He was sixty-two years old and healthy, with a long life in front of him. His money was supposed to provide him and his wife with an income stream for the rest of their lives. Now with the down market and only three years into retirement, he felt he had to go back to work, downsize his home, and sell his second home. He was not positioned properly. A market crash not only impacted his retirement plan but also added stress to his life at a time when he didn't need it.

Unfortunately, there are far too many stories just like this, involving dentists who have retired without locking in guaranteed income streams. Without guarantees in retirement, it only takes one little thing to upset the apple cart, and then the domino effect takes over. It does not have to be this way.

● ● ● ● ● ● ● ● ● ● ● ● ● ● ● ● ● ● ●

Since we have all experienced some setbacks in our financial lives, we need to be proactive and not reactive in casting those setbacks as mere blips on the radar and not devastations. When all contingencies are accounted for in a Financial Treatment Plan, dentists do not have to be reactive when a worst-case scenario occurs, as it is already addressed in their plan. This provides tremendous peace of mind to dentists, as they know they will be okay no matter what happens.

While traditional planners may only talk about the best-case scenario because it is an easier sell, the other factor at work is simply human nature. People are, generally, positive, and we tend to believe that bad things only happen to other people. Unfortunately, when bad things do happen to us, it's too late to make personal preparations. No one has a crystal ball and no matter what we think, life can change at the blink of an eye. We can get in our car today and unintentionally cause an accident by going through a red light that we did not see at an intersection. If that accident causes a disability or death, do you think that will change your financial life? The answer is yes, if you are not properly protected.

As a dentist, whether you have accumulated some wealth at this point in your life or not, you are actually more vulnerable to a lawsuit than the average Joe. Unfortunately, you're a target with a bull's-eye on your back due to having the word *doctor* in front of your name. If a situation such as a car accident were to occur and an attorney were to become involved, you can be certain that you would find yourself in court.

This is where the wrapper or Financial Treatment Plan comes into play. In order for a Financial Treatment Plan to be effective, it must be able to stress-test any conceivable scenario or financial decision. A Financial Treatment Plan allows dentists to measure the impact of a lawsuit, a disability, a premature death, unexpected emergency, and funding for college, to name a few situations. In addition, tax law changes, market fluctuations, and interest rate movements are also measured. The Financial Treatment Plan has the power to measure any one of these variables either by itself or in different combinations.

The Financial Treatment Plan gives us a process whereby we can analyze any decision *before* we actually take action. This is how we can build plans that work under all circumstances. We stress-test situations before implementing them to determine if this is the way we want to go or not. Financial alternatives are tested in the Financial Treatment Plan much as a pilot uses a flight simulator to test different flight situations. It is a proactive process, not reactive. We call it evidence-based financial planning or planning with confidence.

The ability to test and measure different financial scenarios before committing to a financial decision is a difference maker. The Financial Treatment Plan allows dentists to fully measure all of the positive and negative aspects associated with a planning decision and verify expected output on the back end. Another great thing about the Financial Treatment Plan is that dentists can totally customize it to what they want.

A yearly review and update of the dentist's Financial Treatment Plan will help ensure its long-term success. As we discussed earlier, life will change often, and it is important that the Financial Treatment Plan is flexible enough to adapt to any new life changes or events. Changes to the Financial Treatment Plan are simpler to make when the plan is updated annually. On the other hand, drastic decisions may have to be made when yearly reviews are ignored.

Typically, when we meet with dentists, we ask them if there is anything about these wealth objectives that they disagree with. If not, then the next step is to take action and learn more about how the Financial Treatment Plan can be applied in their situation. These objectives become our financial mission statement for everyone we work with. As such, all potential financial decisions are measured against this statement and if they meet its objectives, the dentist will take action of them. If not, they are discarded.

What makes our Financial Treatment Plan unique and different from a traditional financial plan is that the success of our planning process is not dependent upon a magic financial product or investment, or even a single strategy. Also, traditional financial plans fall short by looking at planning considerations such as retirement planning, college planning, debt repayment, and estate planning, to name a few, as individual events. In reality, each of these events affects each other simultaneously. The traditional world has no mechanism like our Financial Treatment Plan to simultaneously measure the impacts of these huge decisions.

In short, financial success is derived from having a Financial Treatment Plan and a rulebook that is based on economic principles in order to measure and analyze financial decisions. It is also imperative that you have a macroadvisor on your team to assist you in sorting through the misinformation, sales hype, and opinion that is rampant in the financial world today. All three need to be present in order to succeed.

We certainly hope these four wealth objectives resonate with you. These are our core values. They enable us to create plans that can work under all circumstances and prevent a pay cut in retirement, which means more life enjoyment.

Chapter 3

EVEN THE LONE RANGER HAD TONTO

• • •

Coaching is taking a player where they can't take themself.

—JOSE MOURINHO

The Lone Ranger was a fictional Western character who fought outlaws with his friend Tonto in the very popular TV series of the same name that ran on ABC from 1949 to 1957. Tonto called the Lone Ranger Kemo Sabe, which means "faithful friend" or "trusty scout." They were a team who fought the bad guys and they needed each other to succeed. Due to all the faulty premises in the world of personal finance, dentists need a faithful and trusted advisor whom they can work with on their journeys toward ultimate financial success. Everyone should have a financial Kemo Sabe!

Dentists graduate from dental school with little to no information or training on how to start a business or manage their money. On top of that, most dental graduates today will likely carry student loan debt in the hundreds of thousands of dollars. Although daunting, you still feel this is a situation you can handle. After all, the fact that you were accepted into dental school proves that you are smart.

The question is, Does this intelligence automatically translate into financial intelligence? From our experience, the answer is no. This is normal, however, because your dental education did not include training in economics or personal finance.

Ask successful athletes what it takes to make it to the next level and they will say a great coach or coaches. Professional athletes use coaches to develop their skills and make them champions. Michael Jordan is the greatest basketball player ever. Tom Brady is the only football player to win six Super Bowls. Serena Williams is the foremost woman tennis player in history. Not one of these athletes achieved their level of success alone. Olympic athletes have multiple coaches. As do professionals in other fields: singers, actors, musicians, CEOs, and entrepreneurs. Even the best dentists have mentors or take continuing education courses to enhance their skills.

So the question should not be, "why do you need help managing your money?" but rather, "why do you think you *don't* need help managing your money?" You may understand basic financial principles, but do you get the nuances? Once your practice is up and running, will you have time to spend monitoring a successful financial plan? You can keep up with your continuing education credits, but do you also have the hours to put into studying new tax laws, reading about the latest financial products, and monitoring the stock market? Are you sure your emotions about money aren't clouding your decisions? Also, are you positive a different perspective won't add to your financial success?

If you are a dentist, you are in the office from eight in the morning until six at night and you are almost always with patients. So when would you have the time to manage your finances? Weekends? Do you really want to spend your weekends pouring over numbers? No you don't, which is why *you* want a coach.

Yet, almost half (46.2 percent) of orthodontists make their own financial decisions and there are websites and blogs that say you should do it yourself. As dentists, we are commonly asked by our patients about techniques and products that they read about online. A lot of that information has no substance or is unfounded, yet people believe it is true because it is on the web. The same goes with personal financial advice. There is a popular blog and website for health professionals that has a course titled "Fire Your Financial Advisor: A Step-By-Step Process to Creating and Implementing Your Own Financial Plan." After finishing our book, you will clearly see that most of the information online and in the media pertaining to financial planning will turn the white coat of the doctor red!

As macroeconomic advisors, our relationship with dental clients is similar to that of a National Football League (NFL) owner with his head coach. The owner brings in a head coach to partner in developing a great team. The head coach holds the ultimate responsibility for putting a winning team on the field. To accomplish this objective, the head coach will work with an offensive coordinator, a defensive coordinator, and a special teams coach. The head coach will also work with other coaches who each specialize in a player position, such as quarterback, lineman, running back, receiver, and others. Together, the efforts of these coaches will build a winning game plan under the direction and leadership of the head coach. It is the head coach's responsibility to make sure that all aspects of the game plan are coordinated so that success can be achieved.

Bringing in those assistant coaches is similar to the macroadvisor working with an accountant, attorney, a bank's lending officer, or investment advisor to build the dentist's financial team. Each one of these microadvisors will be skilled in one or two areas of an individual's personal financial plan, as are the quarterback and defensive line coaches for an NFL team. The microadvisors will bring their ideas to the table, but it is the macroadvisor's job to blend these ideas together to create a game plan for the dentist's financial success. This is similar to the head coach utilizing the skills of his assistant coaches to create a winning team.

A problem we see in the dental world is that financial opinions often get in the way of economic facts, especially if the approach is traditional. Accountants base their opinions about what's financially best for you on their training. The same goes for investment advisors. They are going to focus on investments but don't necessarily see how those investments affect other aspects of your financial life. The ultimate result is skewed in the direction of your advisors' expertise and internal bias. Unfortunately, most dentists will hire an advisor who has the best sales pitch or strongest opinion. Parents, family, and friends of the dentist can also have a lot of influence on their decisions. As tough as it may be, you work very hard for your money. You and your family have to live with the financial decisions you make for the rest of your life, so opinion and sales hype should have no place in your financial plan.

We believe that financial decisions should be based on economic facts, and that all sales hype and opinions should be taken out of the equation. Because there is such a strong emotional attachment to money, this can be very difficult to do, especially if you are presented with information that is incongruent with what you have always thought to be true. A tremendous emotional disconnect is created when something that you always thought to be true is proven not to be. What we present may conflict with the "truths" to which you've been previously exposed. It can be difficult to admit that what you've been doing is not as good as you thought. Making a change means you have to overcome your emotional connection to money and develop the ability to separate facts from opinions.

This is why having a Financial Treatment Plan in your life is so important. Without this key piece as the foundation of your personal finances, it will be extremely difficult to remove emotions from financial decisions. When a Financial Treatment Plan is present in your life, you will have the ability to verify every financial decision based on economics and not sales hype or opinion. Let's examine the framework of the Financial Treatment Plan.

Our Financial Treatment Plan has three components: protection, savings, and growth. Each component has nine individual drawers for a total of twenty-seven drawers. These three components of protection, savings, and growth, as well as debt window and cash flow, are the framework for our game board of finance.

Every dentist develops individualized treatment plans for each patient. When the treatment plan is followed step by step, the end product will always be better than not following a plan. The same applies to our Financial Treatment Plan. When you follow the plan from the top (protection) to the bottom (growth), just as happens with a perfect treatment plan, the result will be a fantastic financial life.

The process is similar to evidence-based dentistry (EBD) where everything that dentists do on their treatment plan is based on science. If you believe in evidence-based dentistry, then how can you not believe in evidence-based financial planning? Ours is the only evidence-based Financial Treatment Plan of its kind.

Let's start with the protection component. The protection component is not where you accumulate wealth. Instead, it is where you protect your wealth so that it doesn't disappear overnight due to some unexpected situation. It is like the moat around a castle. The treasure or investments are held in the castle (savings and growth components) and the moat (protection component) keeps the marauders away.

Protection against unexpected events, such as a lawsuit, or onset of a disability or health issue, are essential. All of these events can and do occur in life; we just can't predict when. Thirty-one percent of orthodontists felt expenses from unexpected life events were a hindrance to being prepared for retirement.[9] If you were faced with any of these situations and had a chance to go back and purchase additional coverage to protect yourself, would you?

For example, if you were in a car accident in which you were clearly at fault, and you could be sued, how much coverage would you buy? You'd want maximum coverage, right? Or if you were disabled by an accident and could go back to the insurance company and add additional disability coverage backdated to the day before you were disabled, how much would you buy? Would you bother to ask about the cost of the premium or would you simply say you want maximum coverage?

With this in mind, if you know you'd want maximum coverage if such an event were to occur, shouldn't you own maximum coverage today even though you *don't know* if the event will occur? The answer is yes! Knowing this, what keeps most dentists from owning maximum protection today? The answer is simple. It is the perceived cost of the insurance premium.

With a Financial Treatment Plan, it is possible for dentists to acquire the protection coverage with little to no out-of-pocket cost to them by recovering expenses lost in the inefficiencies that are present in every traditional financial plan. Money that is already gushing out

---

9   Jeremiah Sturgill and Jae Park, "Changes in Orthodontists' Retirement Planning and Practice Operations Due to the Recent Recession."

of a financial plan can be redirected to carry the amount of coverage a dentist desires, and can do so with minimal to no additional outlay. If that can be done, would there be any reason why you wouldn't want to own maximum protection? Of course not!

The second component in the Financial Treatment Plan is savings. This is where a dentist's safe money resides in the Financial Treatment Plan. Safe money includes, for the most part, both liquid and retirement assets. Liquid assets are comprised of checking, savings, credit union accounts, US savings bonds, CDs, and money market accounts. A dentist's retirement accounts are also included in the savings component and have available the potential tax benefits of tax-deferral, tax-free, and tax-deductible investments. The tax benefits of a retirement account make these accounts the most powerful assets in the savings component.

It is an important to note that retirement plans are positioned in the savings section of the Financial Treatment Plan where safe money resides. Why? Because it is imperative that these funds are still around at the dentist's retirement age. As silly as this may sound, it is critical that retirement funds are invested more conservatively than nonretirement investments. We can't tell you all the horror stories we heard during the market crash of 2008, when retirement funds were invested too aggressively. As a result, when the market crashed, many dentists lost hundreds of thousands to millions of dollars unnecessarily! Since the lion's share of a dentist's total assets for retirement in traditional planning is a combination of 401(k)s and other retirement accounts, a lot of unnecessary pressure is placed on these accounts to perform from a rate-of-return standpoint. As a result, too much risk is assumed in these plans.

Saving provides you with freedom. At the beginning of our career we are all people at work with no money at work. By the end of our career, we want to have all our money at work and no people at work. This objective is only accomplished if we establish discipline in our saving habits.

• • • • • • • • • • • • • • • • • • • •

Mart

If you do not save money, you will *always* have to work. Savings is the fuel that drives a person's Financial Treatment Plan. It is like owning a car. If you want to go anywhere, you first have to put gas in it.

• • • • • • • • • • • • • • • • • • • •

The last component of the Financial Treatment Plan is the growth component. This is where our risk money resides. In this component, the word *safety* is replaced with the word *potential*. The growth component has the potential to deliver income, growth, and tax benefits, but there are no guarantees. Investing is exciting, but it is also risky.

The first layer of the growth component is where we become lenders of our money. We are, basically, lending money to governmental agencies, corporations, or municipalities in the form of a bond. We give them our money when we purchase a bond, and in return, they pay us a stated rate of interest. Our money is returned to us when we either sell the bond or it matures. It sounds safe enough, but there are inherent risks such as credit risk, interest rate risk, and default risk that we need to be aware of, especially in retirement when retirees tend to gravitate toward bonds in their asset allocation.

The second layer of the growth component is where we become investors in corporate America in the form of stock or equity ownership. We can invest in preferred stocks, blue chip stocks, mutual funds, exchange-traded funds (ETFs), or growth stocks. Depending on the type of stock owned, there could be income and/or growth potential realized. Preferred stocks will, typically, have a low growth potential that is offset by their high income potential from dividends paid. On the other end of the spectrum, growth stocks have minimal to zero income potential from dividends paid, but a high growth potential. We like to believe our stock investments will always appreciate in value, but that is not always the case, as we have all experienced!

The third layer of the growth component is where our hard assets are found. This is the highest risk portion of the entire model. Certainly there is potential for high returns, but there is also potential for total loss. Gold, silver, and collections such as art, stamps, or even comic books are considered hard assets. Bitcoin and cryptocurrencies reside in this layer of the Financial Treatment Plan as well, due to their extreme volatility and potential for gain and loss. Other assets in this layer could be a hobby that turns into a business, such as buying and selling antiques or a home business. Real estate is another powerful hard asset. It includes assets such as your personal residence, second home, office building where you practice, and rental property. Finally, the last component of the third layer is tax shelters, such as your dental practice, private equity investments, or captive insurance companies. Your practice is one of the most powerful assets you will own, but it holds a great deal of risk. As a small business owner, Uncle Sam gives you the opportunity to take advantage of some great tax benefits for carrying that risk. Your dental practice is a powerful place to build wealth.

In each component of protection, savings, and growth, the first drawer is the least powerful asset. The last drawer of each component is the most powerful. For example, in the protection component, your car insurance is the least powerful protection asset while your life insurance is the most powerful. In the savings component, your checking account is the least powerful, and the most powerful savings asset is your 401(k) or retirement plan. When you reach the growth component, government bonds are the least powerful and your practice is the most powerful. There is a hierarchy to the model and every insurance and investment product has a specific power and benefit.

Anybody who has played a board game, whether Monopoly, chess, or checkers, knows you have to have a set of rules to go along with the game board in order to play the game. If we just laid out a Monopoly board without the rules, nobody would be able to play. When a set of rules is introduced, however, people understand how to play Monopoly. The same goes for money. To be successful you have to have a game board such as a Financial Treatment Plan and a set of rules that are based on economics. These rules will be explained in chapter 5!

The key to a home standing the test of time is for the home to be built on a solid foundation first and foremost. This is no different when it comes to one's personal finances where the foundation is comprised of a rock-solid protection component. Without this in place your personal finances can and will crumble at some point. Once the protection component is established, the building blocks of the savings and growth components are added to build a Financial Treatment Plan for success. The integration and coordination of these three components, along with the debt window and cash flow, will ensure that your Financial Treatment Plan never develops a crack.

A Financial Treatment Plan built in this manner will provide total peace of mind knowing that, no matter what happens, life is going to be fantastic.

Every financial decision we make has benefits and disadvantages associated with it. As such, they all have to be considered for any financial decision to be properly evaluated. We are not saying that other advisors should not be a part of your financial team, but you need to have a macroadvisor involved to ensure that all of your advisors are on the same page and moving together in the right direction.

A statement we often hear in the dental world, and elsewhere, is that nobody is going to care more about your money than you. We believe this as well. All dentists should be actively engaged with their finances. If dentists try to manage their finances on their own, however, they may run into trouble, due to a lack of knowledge or the time and devotion that managing personal finances effectively requires. Also, dentists acting on their own behalf will certainly not have the Financial Treatment Plan, an essential tool for looking at their entire financial picture. They might be able to function as their own investment advisors, but it may be at the expense of a number of factors in their financial lives that they won't be aware of until it is too late.

Again, there is *no magic product* in the financial arena. We work with the exact same products that everybody else possesses. What is different about our approach is that we focus on the strategy behind the products versus the products themselves. It is the marriage (coordination and integration) of products within the Financial Treatment Plan that creates financial success. That's our winning strategy.

In the end, those dentists who don't have a Financial Treatment Plan create a junk drawer of inefficiency by purchasing products on an as-needed basis. When they are ready to retire, they are left with a bunch of products that are not integrated or coordinated with one another. This disorganization delivers a retirement income that is significantly less than their working income. On the other hand, when you have a *process* that is driven by a Financial Treatment Plan, you can build your retirement to ensure that you will have full income replacement. This means you take no pay cut in your golden years! The time to start your Financial Treatment Plan is *now*, but making that financial journey with a trusted Kemo Sabe at your side is essential!

Chapter 4

MONEY MYTHS DEBUNKED

• • •

Reverse every natural instinct and do the opposite
of what you are inclined to do, and you will probably
come very close to having a perfect golf swing.

—BEN HOGAN

Ben Hogan's advice on reversing "every natural instinct" if you want a successful golf swing can also be applied to financial planning. Do the opposite of what most people recommend and you will come very close to having a perfect financial life. When it comes to financial planning, most of the information available is actually misinformation. The traditional rules of thumb will lead to income insecurity.

Over the years, the rainmakers and their persistent messaging have penetrated our minds to the point that we can't even recognize the difference between financial misinformation and economic truth. The brainwashing of the American public by financial institutions and media runs deep! Nowhere is this brainwashing more prevalent than the promotion of what is touted as successful retirement planning. We always ask if this planning is so good, then why are the vast majority of Americans (78 percent) not prepared for retirement?[10] This statistic pertains to dentists as well, who, on average, retire with only 51 percent of their preretirement income, according to the most recent ADA study on retirement.[11]

Myth can be defined as a widely held but false belief or idea. People struggle financially due to the myths promoted by financial institutions. It is these myths that prevent dentists from becoming financially successful or having full income replacement at retirement. Even the savviest among us buy into these myths. Let's debunk four of the biggest money myths (keep in mind that there are many more).

THE MYTH OF DEBT REPAYMENT

There is a prevailing belief that *all* debt is bad. If you have *any* debt you need to get rid of it as fast as possible. Some pundits even compare debt to a sin. The truth is that not *all* debt is bad debt. There is debt that is good, and if it is managed properly, it can make you wealthier. Bad debt, however, does need to be addressed and understood.

Let's address the bad debt first. This type of debt has high interest rates or interest that is nondeductible. Consumer debt, such as credit card debt, is at the top of that list. You want to get rid of high interest debt as soon as possible. The best way to pay off those credit cards is in the following manner: Arrange your credit card balances from the highest to the lowest. Begin by taking any excess monthly cash flow that can be used for debt reduction and use it to pay off the lowest credit card balance first, regardless of the credit card's interest

---

10   The Data Driven Investor, December 14, 2018.

11   "2010 Survey on Retirement and Investment," American Dental Association.

rate. Once that card is paid off, apply that card's monthly payment (including the excess monthly cash flow) to the next lowest credit card balance until that card balance is paid off. Continue that process until all the credit cards are paid off. This strategy pays off credit card debt very quickly. Also, starting the process with credit cards that have the lowest balance gives you emotional momentum to continue chipping off the debt more quickly.

If you have car loans or other consumer debt with high interest rates, try and eliminate them as quickly as possible in the same manner. However, if you have a car note that carries a 0 percent or 1.9 percent interest rate, there is no reason to accelerate that debt repayment as those funds can be better used elsewhere. This is why it is important to look at each debt individually.

Contrary to what many of the radio pundits preach today, even in churches across America, there actually is such a thing as good debt. One type of good debt is a properly structured mortgage. The reason for this is twofold. First, mortgage interest is still one of the few tax deductions available (although the Tax Reform Act of 2018 somewhat lessened this deduction).

Second, you should also consider how inflation impacts a mortgage payment over time. Inflation is your friend when it comes to mortgage loans. Today is the only day that your dollar is worth 100 cents. As time goes on, inflation will dramatically decrease the value of that dollar. As an example, if you pay cash for your home today, in essence you have used dollars valued at 100 cents to pay off your mortgage. If you take a thirty-year mortgage out to purchase your home, you will purchase your home with 360 fixed monthly payments over thirty years. Every year you have that mortgage, you are paying the financial institution back with cheaper dollars due to the impact of inflation. At a 3 percent inflation rate, in the fifteenth year, you are using dollars worth only sixty-four cents to make your mortgage payment. At the end of thirty years, the dollars you use to pay the mortgage will only be worth forty-one cents!

Low interest rates also make mortgages attractive, especially when they are tax-deductible. It is almost like free money in a low-interest-rate environment. Even if mortgage rates are 5 percent, that is still a low rate.

When structuring your mortgage, you want a mortgage term that is fixed for as long as possible, such as thirty years, not fifteen years. Also, you definitely don't want an adjustable rate mortgage (ARM). That interest rate will adjust annually after a fixed interest rate period of five to seven years. An ARM in certain situations can work if the homeowner is going to be out of the house before the ARM reaches the end of its fixed term (e.g., the homeowner has a seven-year ARM and intends to stay in the home no longer than five years). When people intend to stay in their home for the long term, an ARM does not make a lot of sense, especially if interest rates are low. In this situation, you could expose yourself to higher interest rates when the mortgage adjusts, as you have no control over mortgage rates in the future.

An ARM mortgage can unnecessarily expose an individual to future interest rate risk. The term length of your debt should match the longevity of the asset being purchased. In the case of purchasing a home, a fixed-rate, thirty-year mortgage is most likely your best option.

With this information in mind, let's break down the three most common ways to pay for a home. In this example, we will examine the efficiency of either paying cash outright or using a fifteen- or thirty-year mortgage to acquire the residence. The facts related to this home purchase are:

Purchase price: $500,000

Down payment: 20 percent, or $100,000

Mortgage rate options: fifteen-year loan at 4.50 percent; thirty-year loan at 4.75 percent

Personal federal tax bracket: 30 percent

Cost of money (opportunity cost): 6 percent

Analysis period: 360 months (30 years)

The financial world we live in today promotes the idea that paying cash, or at the very least accelerating the repayment of a mortgage, is the best way to purchase a house. After all, if you were to pay cash for your home, no mortgage interest would be incurred. In contrast, if you have a thirty-year mortgage in this scenario, you would pay a whopping $351,172 of interest over thirty years. We have all been told that paying interest on debt is bad, and we should avoid it, or at the very least, find a way to minimize this expense. Most individuals don't have the cash reserves available to pay cash for a home, so the next best alternative for them, in order to avoid high interest costs, is to accept a fifteen-year mortgage instead. In this example, the interest costs for a fifteen-year mortgage are $150,795. See table 4.1 on the next page for a summary of these results.

MORTGAGE OPTIONS	DOWN PAYMENT	MORTGAGE PAYMENT	CUMULATIVE INTEREST
Cash	$500,000	-0-	-0-
15-year loan	$100,000	$3,060	$150,795
30-year loan	$100,000	$2,087	$351,172

Table 4.1

At this point, if we base our decision on how we pay for a home solely on the potential interest costs incurred, then paying cash or opting for a shorter-term mortgage makes all the sense in the world. A thirty-year mortgage would make no sense at all due to the higher interest costs.

This is the exact reasoning you will hear from traditional financial advisors, bankers, and the various financial entertainers advising you on the TV and radio, and in the print media. Their analysis of how you should pay for a home is based solely on interest costs incurred and does not look at the complete picture. There are other factors that have to be considered in looking at how you should pay for a home. The two biggest factors overlooked by traditional financial advisors are individual opportunity cost (cost of money) and the benefit of any tax savings generated from a potential mortgage-interest tax deduction.

Opportunity cost, which is never considered in the traditional world of planning, is a key concept in economics. The *New Oxford American Dictionary* defines opportunity cost as "the loss of potential gain from other alternatives when one alternative is chosen." In this case, every dollar used to purchase a home, including cash up front or the remittance of monthly mortgage payments over time, generates an opportunity cost as these dollars could have been used for an alternative investment. In our analysis, we have assigned an opportunity cost of 6 percent (see table 4.2).

MORTGAGE OPTIONS	(A) COMPOUNDED PRINCIPAL AND INTEREST	CUMULATIVE TAX SAVINGS	(B) COMPOUNDED TAX SAVINGS	(A–B) NET COMPOUND MORTGAGE COST
Cash	$3,011,288	-0-	-0-	$3,011,288
15-year loan	$2,786,149	$45,239	$202,625	$2,583,524
30-year loan	$2,698,268	$105,352	$356,842	$2,341,426

Table 4.2

The compounded principal and interest amount for a cash purchase in this example totals $3,011,288 after thirty years. This amount simply represents the original $500,000 cash payment for the house, invested at 6 percent over thirty years in an alternative investment. The most cost-effective way to purchase the home was accomplished with a thirty-year mortgage. The compounded principal and interest amount of $2,698,268 represents a 6 percent alternative investment in which an initial deposit of $100,000 and 360 monthly contributions of $2,087 were made.

Another factor that comes into play is the potential mortgage-interest tax deduction on the loan. The cumulative tax savings generated from this tax deduction and the related opportunity costs must be measured and netted out of the compound mortgage loan cost as well. When all economic factors are measured macroeconomically, it is rare that anything less than a thirty-year mortgage makes sense.

• • • • • • • • • • • • • • • • • • •

Mart

We have found in almost every client situation that a thirty-year mortgage is the most cost effective way to purchase a home. Having a thirty-year mortgage does not mean that it cannot be paid off in a shorter period of time if that makes sense. Finally, it is important to remember that a home appreciates at the same rate whether the property has a mortgage against it or not.

• • • • • • • • • • • • • • • • • • •

• • • • • • • • • • • • • • • • • • •

Tim

Another way to think of this mortgage dilemma is to examine the situation of two dentists. Dentist A has a half-million-dollar home that is free and clear with no other assets or debt. This means his net worth is $500,000. Dentist B also has a net worth of $500,000, comprised of a half-million-dollar home with a $250,000 mortgage and cash of $250,000 ($500,000 home + $250,000 cash minus $250,000 mortgage = $500,000).

Which dentist would you rather be? Dentist A, who has a debt-free home and zero cash in his model, or Dentist

B, who has a $500,000 home with a $250,000 mortgage and $250,000 in cash?

Could Dentist B pay off his mortgage tomorrow and be in the exact same position as Dentist A? Of course, he could. So, in reality, Dentist B is debt-free but with more wealth-building options. For example, if the interest rate environment is one where CD rates are paying 10–12 percent (as in the early 1980s, see Bankrate.com), and Dentist B has a mortgage locked in at 4 percent, why would he use his cash to pay off his mortgage when he could invest it in a CD and earn substantially more interest? In this situation, as emotionally satisfying as it may be to be debt-free, nobody who wants to be wealthier would pay off the mortgage and possibly lose the tax deduction if a safe CD could more than triple that cash. Not even a radio personality would do this!

Now some of you may be thinking that Dentist A could also do the same thing by pulling money out of his home via a new mortgage or home equity line of credit (HELOC) to invest in the CD. That could certainly be done, but if CD rates are at 10 percent, you can be certain that interest rates for a new mortgage, or HELOC, will be higher as well. Would you pull money out of your home at 12 percent to invest it in a 10 percent CD? This does not make sense, even though a 10 percent CD is fantastic. What this comes down to is that those who win have more control of their cash.

The point is that cash flow is king. Whoever has the cash gets to make the rules and is in control. If you do not have control of your cash, you are subject to the whims of others.

• • • • • • • • • • • • • • • • • • • •

Some of our initial principles in the Financial Treatment Plan are aimed at getting your annual savings rate up to 15 percent or more and building a liquidity position equal to 50 percent of one year's gross household income. If you are focused solely on eliminating all of your debt before you do anything else, it will take significantly longer to have that liquidity in place, a move that would be financially dangerous. If you're throwing everything you have into paying off your debt, you'll be in trouble if a situation were to arise that demands funds and you have no liquidity to address that situation. You're paying off debt at the expense of liquidity.

When you throw all of your excess cash flow into debt reduction, you forgo other opportunities that may provide you with better investment returns and benefits. In the end, improperly paying off debt means fewer income streams in retirement as well, which usually means you will be working longer. This is why it is financially unhealthy to focus on debt repayment from a linear viewpoint (microviewpoint), as it will make you poorer.

For instance, if you pay off your house in ten years, you may think you've made a great decision. After all, this is what your traditional advisors or parents have advised you to do. You may be thinking that you will be mortgage-free in ten years and will have saved thousands of dollars in mortgage interest over a thirty-year mortgage. However, macroeconomically, it could be the wrong decision because the monies that went toward that mortgage repayment might have been better used elsewhere, as, for example, in investments or insurance. Also, and maybe more importantly, what other benefits did you give up by prematurely locking your money up in the equity of your home?

Another good debt is a student loan. As a dentist, you might not have been able to pursue your career without incurring that debt. Student loan debt is an *investment,* not a *cost.* It's an investment in your career, but it needs to be managed properly. You want your loan terms fixed and you want to be in control of it. Some student loan repayments are based on a dentist's income, which frequently makes the loan a negative amortizing note. This means that even though you are making payments, the loan balance is still going up. That's a future train wreck. It is imperative that dentists amortize student loans as quickly as possible upon graduation. Also, for cash flow purposes, larger loans should, initially, be amortized for as long as possible.

We acknowledge this is a different way of looking at debt, but quite frankly, you must have the training and the degree to practice as a dentist and earn a lot of money. That degree is going to allow you to earn hundreds of thousands of dollars a year. If you come out of school with a debt of $200,000–300,000 or more, that is your buy-in to a career that will deliver substantial income to you over your lifetime.

• • • • • • • • • • • • • • • • • • •

Tim

If you were able to start contributing $50,000 a year to your 401(k) plan at age thirty and you continued doing this for the next thirty-five years, at a 6 percent rate of return, you would have accumulated $5.9 million by age sixty-five. If you were, instead, to delay your $50,000 contribution to a 401(k) plan by ten years (and begin contributing at age forty) because you were initially concentrating on paying off your debt, then, at age sixty-five, you would have only $2.9 million at a 6 percent rate of return. You lost three million dollars of potential wealth because you were focused solely on eliminating debt, directing excess cash flow to that objective before starting a retirement plan.

I am totally on board with getting rid of consumer debt and high-interest credit-card debt, but to make a blanket statement that all debt has to be eliminated is shooting yourself in the foot.

• • • • • • • • • • • • • • • • • • • •

In conclusion, if you can amortize your good loans at a low interest rate, receive a tax deduction, and let inflation be your friend over time, you will realize the double benefit of maintaining control *and* flexibility of your money over the course of your loan.

THE MYTH OF FUNDING THE RETIREMENT PLAN TO THE MAXIMUM

All our new clients have been advised by their accountant or financial advisor to fund their retirement plan at the maximum level if they want to have a successful retirement. Typically, the recommendation is a 401(k) safe harbor plan that includes a profit-sharing contribution. This means that, for most dentists, the majority of their savings are going into a retirement plan. As with all financial products, however, 401(k) plans have advantages and disadvantages that need to be evaluated.

A fallacy that is often repeated in traditional financial planning circles is that contributors to a tax-deductible retirement plan such as a 401(k) are saving taxes. There are *no* tax savings on this contribution! Instead, contributors only receive a tax deduction for their contribution today with a tax deferral on future growth. In the future, ordinary income taxes will be paid on withdrawals. As a result, there is an embedded tax in every tax-deductible retirement plan. The only way you will receive a tax savings from such a plan is if you happen to be in a lower tax bracket when you retire. If this occurs, due to taking a pay cut in retirement, then your advisor has failed you because you will have less income to enjoy in your golden years.

When dentists fill out a balance sheet for their lenders or themselves, they list their checking, savings, investments, and retirement plans as assets. When they list their liabilities, however, they never itemize the corresponding tax liability that is due on their retirement plan. As a result, every personal balance sheet is overstated from a net worth standpoint.

Dentists never take this into account until it is brought to their attention. The Securities and Exchange Commission (SEC) would never allow a business to only list the value of their assets and not state their corresponding liabilities, whether current or deferred, yet it is accepted in the personal finance arena. With this in mind, most personal financial statements are not accurate.

Although the payment of this embedded tax in the retirement plan is deferred to some unknown point in the future, it is still a real cost that must be recognized. Keep in mind that the cost of this deferred tax will increase if, at the time of withdrawal, you are in a higher tax bracket than the tax bracket you were in at the time of your original deferral rate. You will pay that tax at some point in time and tax rates have continuously changed throughout history (see the following

Bradford Tax Institute graph). The compounding that occurs as part of a retirement plan may not generate the same compound tax impact that occurs in an after-tax investment during growth years, but it is not free. You will pay that tax later in life. There is no free lunch!

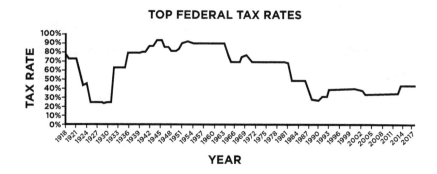

Bradford Tax Institute Graph

Figure 4.1

There are positive things about a traditional retirement plan. The money goes in before tax and it grows, tax-deferred, until you withdraw it at retirement. There are also some negative things that must be considered. The biggest negative issue is that once your money goes in, under present tax laws, it is locked up until you are at least the age of fifty-nine and a half. If you take money out before then, you will pay a 10 percent premature distribution penalty, plus ordinary income taxes on the money at that time. Accessing your own money from a retirement plan prior to the age of fifty-nine and a half is very costly. There is a way for limited access to these funds without penalty prior to age fifty-nine and a half, but you must follow very specific IRS guidelines to accomplish this.

Another drawback to having money in a retirement plan is that you have no control over these assets other than where you may invest them. It is important to keep in mind who is responsible for making all of the rules for retirement plans. In this instance, the rainmaker is the federal government. The government tells us how much money we can put into our retirement plans and when we can take funds out. It also dictates the tax rate we will pay at the time of withdrawal. Unfortunately, this rate is subject to change as tax laws are revised with each newly elected congress.

Another huge consideration that is never discussed when making a retirement contribution is the fact that government can change the age of withdrawal. Let's assume that you want to retire at age sixty, which many dentists do. You may get within two years of retirement and the government could change the withdrawal age to sixty-five or sixty-seven. How excited would you be about your money sitting in a retirement plan, knowing that you will have to work longer in order to get the money out penalty-free? If you think that can't happen, think again. There has already been talk of extending the withdrawal age to as late as age seventy. If this actually came to pass, would that affect how you would save for retirement?

● ● ● ● ● ● ● ● ● ● ● ● ● ● ● ● ● ● ●

Tim

Years ago you could access money held in a retirement plan at any age without penalty. Since then, the government has implemented a minimum age requirement of fifty-nine and a half for withdrawal, which an investor must adhere to in order to avoid an early withdrawal penalty. My point is this: the government is always looking for ways to force people to work for a longer period of time, not a shorter one. This statement is also supported by the fact that the government has gradually extended the age to receive full Social Security benefits to age sixty-seven for those born in 1960 or later. They also further reduced the Social Security benefits for those retiring as early as age sixty-two. I believe that the government fully recognizes the fact that their tax revenue base relies more on working people than retired people.

• • • • • • • • • • • • • • • • • • • •

When we look at retirement, we include everything in the Financial Treatment Plan, not just a 401(k) plan, which is only one drawer of the model. Why can't your retirement plan include a 401(k) plan as well as other assets such as after-tax investments, municipal bonds, income-producing real estate, and a business that you build and sell? Your retirement plan should include all of these things and more, not just a 401(k).

Dentists, typically, have three buckets from which to pull income during retirement: Social Security, their 401(k), and the sale of their practice. The 401(k) is the primary investment vehicle for 60 percent of orthodontists.[12] When the *whole* Financial Treatment Plan is used as the retirement plan, rather than being limited to these three buckets, dentists have the opportunity to add another five to eight income streams in retirement. Having multiple income streams in retirement adds diversification to the overall retirement income and retirees are no longer dependent on any one income source, which adds peace of mind to their retirement. As was mentioned earlier, successful Americans have at least seven income streams in retirement, and you should too. We call this diversifying your income streams.

---

12   Jeremiah Sturgill and Jae Park, "Changes in Orthodontists' Retirement Planning and Practice Operations Due to the Recent Recession."

Recall our earlier example of contributing $50,000 to a 401(k) for thirty-five years at 6 percent to generate $5.9 million by retirement. Many dentists look at that number and think, *Great! My retirement is done.* The problem is, however, no matter how big the final number, every financial decision has a cost. A retirement plan is no different. These costs may not be fully disclosed, but they still exist. When we look at a 401(k) plan or a profit-sharing plan, there are always embedded costs.

• • • • • • • • • • • • • • • • • • • •

Mart

Dentist A is setting up a 401(k) plan. In order for Dentist A to fully participate in the 401(k), she will have to provide a safe harbor match for her employees. This match will oftentimes range from 3 to 4 percent of their wages. Assuming staff wages of $250,000 and a 4 percent match, this amounts to a $10,000 employer contribution that Dentist A will make each year. Now, this match may be viewed by the staff as a great employee benefit and may, ultimately, be an incentive for employees to remain with Dentist A's practice long-term. Nonetheless, we have to recognize the match as an annual cost to Dentist A's practice.

In addition, there are administrative fees associated with the 401(k) plan. Typically, they will run anywhere from $4,000 to $5,000 a year. Assuming Dentist A contributes a match of $10,000 plus administrative fees of $4,000, Dentist A's annual costs for the 401(k) plan are $14,000 each year. Over twenty-five years, her total out-of-pocket costs will amount to $350,000. If a discretionary profit-sharing contribution is made each year in order for Dentist A to fully maximize her contribution to the 401(k), these costs are only increased. They could easily exceed well over a half a million dollars, in total, over time.

No matter how much money Dentist A makes, this is a lot of money! Unfortunately, this is only part of the story when it comes to plan costs; there is also an opportunity cost on the $14,000 paid annually for the 401(k) plan. If these monies were not paid out and instead retained in Dentist A's Financial Treatment Plan, they could have been invested for her benefit. For example, if she had invested the annual costs of $14,000 at 6 percent over twenty-five years, they would have grown to be $814,000. This is the real cost of sponsoring a 401(k) plan, and it must be considered when looking at a 401(k) plan.

Again, we are not saying that a 401(k) should not be part of a dentist's overall retirement strategy. After all, according to our economic rules of wealth building (discussed in the next chapter), it should be. Thus a 401(k) has a place in overall wealth building. However, we encourage dentists not to simply fall in line with the rest of the herd, who are being led over a cliff by the traditional financial world. Financial advisors who indiscriminately promote to dentists the full funding of a safe harbor 401(k) plan at more than $50,000 annually (or worse yet, a cash balance plan that may allow a dentist to add upward of $200,000 or more to retirement accounts) do great harm. These plans have real costs, which you need to know before committing to sponsoring a 401(k). Once plan costs are identified, it's important to look at how those costs can be minimized or, better yet, recaptured over time.

• • • • • • • • • • • • • • • • • • • •

Let's look at another piece of traditional retirement advice, which involves putting your spouse on the payroll with a salary of more than $25,000 a year. This is oftentimes recommended for the sole purpose of allowing the spouse to make a maximum contribution of $19,000 (for those under the age of fifty) to a 401(k) plan. Again, more money going into the 401(k) will make the retirement numbers look bigger in the end, but at what cost? By placing a spouse on the payroll, the dentist has taken income that may have been distributed to the family as unearned income via a bonus or distribution and turned it into earned income, which is now subject to FICA payroll taxes of 15.3 percent. The FICA payroll taxes on a salary of $25,000 are $3,825. These additional payroll taxes literally represent what is, in essence, a 20 percent front-end load (charge) in order for your spouse to put $19,000 into a 401(k) plan.

Stop and think about it. If we said, "We've got a great investment that allows you to contribute $19,000 each year to an account, but it has a front-end load of 20 percent," how excited would you be to put money into that investment? We are fairly certain that you wouldn't do it. Yet, for spouses who are on the payroll for the sole purpose of making a retirement contribution, this is an annual front-end load as FICA taxes are paid on the spouse's salary every year!

Instead of placing your spouse on the payroll, and incurring a cost of almost $24,000 (consisting of the 401(k) contribution of

$19,000, a safe harbor match, and the FICA taxes paid of $3,825), consider buying a second home. Use the $24,000 ($2,000 per month) to pay toward the monthly mortgage on a second home. Now you can actually live in your 401(k), so to speak, and create lasting memories with your family and friends today. What is the rate of return on enjoyment when creating memories with your family? We actually believe that it can't be measured, as it is infinite. Most certainly it is far greater than any paper return on a retirement plan that will provide you no enjoyment until you retire. Also keep in mind that the appreciation on the real estate is taxed at capital gain rates, whereas the gains in a retirement plan are taxed as ordinary income when withdrawn from the plan.

As mentioned in chapter 2, the ownership of a second home may provide additional tax deductions in the form of mortgage interest and real estate taxes paid. These deductions were limited, however, with the passing of the Tax Cuts and Jobs Act of 2017. Also, depending on the property's location, it could become an income-producing rental property when the family is not using it. Another benefit of renting out the property is that you can deduct any expenses for the property maintenance and upkeep. (Please consult an accountant for all tax deductions.)

Financial institutions, corporations, and the government promulgate the traditional money myths we cling to. It goes back to the three entities, or rainmakers, we identified earlier that are fighting for our money. Almost twenty-five trillion dollars are held in retirement funds in America today.[13] The financial institutions are managing these monies and charging fund fees, management fees, and advisory

---

13   Nick Thornton, "Total retirement assets near $25 trillion mark," Benefits
      PRO, June 30, 2015, https://www.benefitspro.com/2015/06/30/
      total-retirement-assets-near-25-trillion-mark.

fees. Is it to their benefit to discourage people from contributing to these plans? Also, do they encourage people to withdraw money from their retirement accounts to spend and enjoy? The answer is no, because that diminishes the fee income these financial institutions receive each year.

Instead, they tell us to throw all of our money into retirement accounts so that we can retire. When we get to retirement age, they tell us that "to avoid a big tax burden on any money withdrawn from the account, you should defer withdrawals from the retirement plan until seventy and a half years old." When we reach age seventy and a half, we are then told that in order to further avoid or minimize taxes, we should only take out the required minimum distribution (RMD), which starts at about 3.6 percent of the account balance. Well, that's great! You poured all this money into a retirement plan during your working years only to continue deferring it when you initially retire. Then when you do finally take distributions from your retirement plan at seventy and a half, you set yourself up to take minimum distributions from the plan. Why would you not want to have maximum distributions from your retirement plan from day one of retirement? In the traditional world, if you only take RMD distributions from your retirement plan, you may very well decrease your tax burden, but you will most certainly reduce your enjoyment of life in retirement.

● ● ● ● ● ● ● ● ● ● ● ● ● ● ● ● ● ● ● ●

Mart

There are large dental advisory firms across the country that charge dentists an annual fee of $5,000 to $25,000 *per year* for planning services. If the dental advisory firm also manages investments for their clients, then those clients will also pay investment fees to that firm. In this case, a dentist is actually paying double for the firm's services. These advisors cost their clients millions of dollars of lost wealth through these additional and unnecessary fees. Dentists often think they're getting great advice because they're paying a planning fee. That money, however, is pulled from the dentist's pockets never to return. Instead, the money is enriching the advisor at the expense of the dentist.

● ● ● ● ● ● ● ● ● ● ● ● ● ● ● ● ● ● ● ●

As if the costs to have a retirement plan were not bad enough already, let's analyze the impact of investment advisory fees that are paid out to financial advisors. Again, back to the example where we talked about saving $50,000 into a retirement plan for thirty-five years. If we assume a 1 percent advisory fee over thirty-five years, the advisor will collect $593,000 in fees over those thirty-five years. Because these fees are netted out of the account results (*netting* means "taking the fees from the account directly"), your account balance at age sixty-five will approximate $4.7 million and not the $5.9 million originally projected. You want to talk about wealth erosion? That 1 percent advisory fee just cost you $1.2 million in terms of the accumulation value of your account.

Unfortunately, most people are paying an investment advisory fee that is greater than 1 percent. This is eye opening to say the least. Fees have to be paid to the advisor, but it is essential to keep them as low as possible. Better yet, the advisor should build cost recovery strategies into the Financial Treatment Plan to fully recover these fees. This is ideal planning!

We want you to learn to focus on obtaining multiple uses of the same dollar, rather than only getting a singular use from each dollar over your lifetime. Money that goes into a retirement plan counts as one use for that dollar. Once that dollar is in that plan, it's trapped until you are at least age fifty-nine and a half. If you're going to put money into a retirement plan, why not run it through another area of your Financial Treatment Plan first so that by the time that dollar goes into your retirement plan, you will be getting a second or third use from it? That way you get two or three uses out of the same dollar and create additional benefits and money supply before that dollar is locked up in a retirement account.

A final thought on retirement plans is from a tax and estate planning perspective. Do you really want to die with all your money stuck in a retirement plan that only benefits and enriches the financial institutions? The answer to this question should be an unequivocal no. Funds left in a retirement plan at death may be subject to huge tax consequences. Also, keep in mind that tax laws change and will continue to do so. When everything is considered, we often find that dentists' retirement funds should be spent first (not last) so they can fully enjoy their money while they are alive.

The decision to fund a retirement plan is an important one, but understanding the many moving parts of these plans has a significant impact on your future retirement income. A lack of understanding will result in less income in your golden years. Knowing the advantages and disadvantages of these plans will position you for full income replacement in retirement!

THE MYTH OF TERM LIFE INSURANCE

Of all the insurance coverage we purchase throughout our lifetime, there is only one that we are guaranteed to use and that is life insurance! Why? Because we are mortal and dying is a natural part of life. Since dying is guaranteed, doesn't it make sense to have it until that time? This may sound like common sense, yet very few people have life insurance in force when they die.

Let's start here: Term life insurance is a product no one uses. If you qualify for term insurance today, the chances of your loved ones collecting a death benefit on that policy are less than 1 percent.[14] Yes, less than 1 percent! Why? Because term life insurance is priced to expire before *you* expire.

Through the life underwriting process, life insurance companies can determine with great accuracy your life expectancy. Unexpected events or accidents aside, the insured will outlive their term insurance 99 percent of the time. As a result, most people pay term premiums to an insurance company for a policy that will never pay a death benefit, due to the fact that the term policy either expired or has been dropped long before the person dies. This is what makes it such a great product for insurance companies. It is the most profitable form of life insurance that an insurance company can sell. Wouldn't it be great to sell an insurance product in which there is less than a 1 percent chance of ever having to pay a claim? The sale of term life insurance is a license to print money for the insurance companies.

---

14 Doug Mitchell, "Why Term Life Insurance Is Cheaper," BestLifequote, February 12, 2019, https://www.bestlifequote.com/blog/cheap-term-life-insurance.

(On a side note, the least profitable form of life insurance sold is whole life insurance.)

Every advisor, including us, will tell you that you should have some form of life insurance. Term life insurance, on the surface, appears to be the most cost-effective way to purchase life insurance. From a macroeconomic standpoint, however, it's the most expensive form of life insurance a person will ever own. The reason for this is that the cost of term insurance *never* ends!

People are led to believe that the cost of term insurance is limited to the total premiums paid and that the costs stop when the policy is canceled. The true total cost of term insurance is threefold: it includes 1) the total premiums paid over the insured's lifetime, plus 2) the opportunity costs on the term premiums paid until the insured's death, and 3) ultimately, the lost death benefit that is never paid out at death to a surviving spouse, children, and future generations. The true cost of term insurance to families will total hundreds of thousands and oftentimes millions of dollars over the insured's lifetime. Let's look at a common example:

Insured's current age: thirty-five

Age at death: eighty-five

Death benefit: $1,000,000

Level term period: thirty years

Annual premium: $700

Cost of money (opportunity cost): 6 percent

The traditional financial world has trained us to view the cost of term insurance as only the total amount of premiums paid. In this example, if we had a thirty-year level term policy with an annual premium of $700, our total cost for the term would be $21,000 over thirty years. At the end of thirty years, the premium would cease and the death benefit of $1,000,000 would go away.

In reality, though, the premiums paid could have been invested and earned interest. At a 6 percent opportunity cost, the premiums paid over thirty years would have grown to $58,661 if invested instead. This is a significant cost with no ultimate benefit as the death benefit is completely lost at the end of the level term period.

OPPORTUNITY COST OF 30-YEAR TERM INSURANCE

Annual payment: $700

Interest rate: 6 percent

Number of years: 30

FUTURE VALUE: $58,661

Unfortunately, the cost of the term will not cease just because you stop paying premiums. The expense of $58,661 for lost premiums and interest at the end of thirty years will continue to accrue lost earnings for the rest of that individual's lifetime. If this person were to live another twenty years to age eighty-five, the total cost of premiums paid and lost earnings would amount to $188,134. This lost wealth was, essentially, transferred to the insurance company as it collected